STUDY GUIDE

James J. Teevan
University of Western Ontario

INTRODUCTION TO SOCIOLOGY
A Canadian Focus

Seventh Edition

Edited by
James J. Teevan
W. E. Hewitt

Toronto

© 2001 Pearson Education Canada Inc., Toronto, Ontario

All rights reserved. This publication is protected by copyright, and permission should be obtained from the publisher prior to any prohibited reproduction, storage in a retrieval system, or transmission in any form or by any means, electronic, mechanical, photocopying, recording or likewise. For information regarding permission, write to the Permissions Department.

ISBN 0-13-030557-X

Acquisitions Editor: Jessica Mosher
Developmental Editor: Lisa Phillips
Production Editor: Sherry Torchinsky
Production Coordinator: Wendy Moran

3 4 5   04 03 02

Printed and bound in Canada.

Contents

Preface		v
Chapter 1	What is Sociology?	1
Chapter 2	Research Methods	7
Chapter 3	Culture	15
Chapter 4	Socialization	22
Chapter 5	Deviance	31
Chapter 6	Social Stratification	38
Chapter 7	Gender Relations	46
Chapter 8	Race and Ethnic Relations	53
Chapter 9	Aging	60
Chapter 10	Families	65
Chapter 11	Religion	73
Chapter 12	Media	80
Chapter 13	Work and Organizations	86
Chapter 14	Social Movements	92
Chapter 15	Demography and Urbanization	100
Chapter 16	Social Change	107

Preface

This *Study Guide* is designed for use with the seventh edition of *Introduction to Sociology: A Canadian Focus*, James J. Teevan and W.E. (Ted) Hewitt, editors. It provides students with study aids that complement the text.

For each chapter the following are included:

1. *Chapter objectives:* a brief overview.
2. *Key terms and definitions.*
3. *Self-quiz:* multiple choice questions.
4. *Fill in the blanks:* a further set of questions to facilitate learning.
5. *Answers*: to all of the questions.

CHAPTER 1

What is Sociology?

OBJECTIVES

1. To define sociology and be able to distinguish it from other social sciences.

2. To be familiar with the historical background that led to the development of the discipline.

3. To understand the major theoretical positions taken by sociologists to explain human interaction, including functionalist, conflict, symbolic-interactionist, and feminist perspectives.

4. To be familiar with the historical development of Canadian sociology.

KEY TERMS AND DEFINITIONS

1. _____: social sources or causes of behaviour used by sociologists to explain rates of behaviour in groups as opposed to individual behaviour.

2. _____: the microsociological argument that individuals act and interact based on their past history of associations, rewards and punishments, and observing and being instructed by others.

3. _____: the sociological model that portrays society as harmonious and as based on consensus.

4. _____: the microsociological view that individuals act on the basis of what they expect will help them to achieve their goals, and interact by playing cooperative and non-cooperative games with each other.

5. _____: the sociological model that argues that individuals subjectively define and interpret their environments, that they are not fully constrained, and that they act from reasons rather than causes.

6. _____: the understanding as opposed to the predicting of behaviour.

7. _____: the sociological model which portrays society as marked by competition and/or exploitation.

8. _____: the occasional minor, temporary disruptions in social life, as defined by functionalists.

9. _____: seen by functionalist as the normal state of society, one marked by interdependence of parts and by harmony and consensus.

SELF-QUIZ

1. One of the major concerns of sociology is
   a) to explain individual sources of behaviour
   b) cultural transmission and cultural uniformity
   c) to explain how membership in social groups affects individual behaviour
   d) deviant behaviour
   e) to study the production and consumption of resources

2. Social facts are
   a) individual internal sources of behaviour
   b) factors pertaining to group structures or to the interrelationships between individuals in groups
   c) factors that may exist outside individual consciousness
   d) factors that help people learn the content of a culture
   e) b and c

3. The type of suicide that men, Protestants, older people, and single people are more likely to commit is
   a) fatalistic suicide
   b) egoistic suicide
   c) altruistic suicide
   d) anomic suicide
   e) alienated suicide

4. Feminist approaches include each of the following, except:
   a) an examination of gender as one variable among many
   b) looking at the informal and hidden aspects of social life
   c) an examination of gender roles
   d) a more interdisciplinary approach
   e) acceptance of a variety of sociological models

5. Scientific explanations can be characterized by the following:
   a) intuition and faith
   b) empirical testing and explanations of unique events
   c) causal statements and common sense
   d) simplicity and predictive ability
   e) all of the above

6. Fatalistic suicide is most likely to occur in societies in which
   a) there are insufficient rules and regulations
   b) the regulations concerning sexual behaviour are lax
   c) there is enormous variation and conflict with regard to the content of norms, values, and roles
   d) people feel trapped, with insufficient alternatives
   e) b and c

7. Which of the following statements is not part of the functionalist perspective?
   a) large and complex societies are similar in structure to the human body
   b) social change is gradual and for the improvement of society
   c) the existence of cultural universals helps societies remain in equilibrium
   d) social arrangements persist because they benefit society
   e) society is marked by peace and consensus

8. Feminist sociology is least likely to take ideas from
   a) symbolic interactionism
   b) conflict sociology
   c) functionalism
   d) anglophone sociology
   e) francophone sociology

9. Scientific explanations should be simple, parsimonious, and elegant. Parsimonious means
   a) admirable, as with a work of art
   b) generalizing rather than unique
   c) empirical; they are synonyms
   d) explaining the most with the least
   e) more pure than applied

10. Symbolic interactionism focuses on
    a) a macro-level of analysis
    b) the place of art in society
    c) cultural integration
    d) the autonomy of individuals
    e) group constraints

11. Weber, more than Durkheim, believed that sociology should include
    a) linguistic relativism
    b) subjective states of the individual
    c) mechanical solidarity
    d) a and c
    e) b and c

12. *Verstehen* is most closely associated with
    a) functionalism
    b) structural functionalism
    c) conflict theory
    d) equilibrium
    e) symbolic interactionism

FILL IN THE BLANKS

1. Durkheim believed that to understand behaviour, one must not only look at individual factors but also at such things as integration or the amount of regulation in society, factors he called _____.

2. The first question of feminist sociology is always _____?

3. Sociology is the study of social behaviour and relationships. It examines the effects of society and _____ upon human behaviour. Therefore, sociologists generally talk about _____ rates and _____ differences.

4. One result of the French and Industrial Revolutions was that simple, small, rural societies, which were based upon tradition, became more _____ and _____, conditions which fostered the growth of sociology.

5. Auguste Comte, who is considered by some the founder of sociology, saw sociology as a secular religion as well as a science, with sociologists as _____.

6. Symbolic interactionists are more interested in _____ behaviour than in _____ behaviour.

7. The functionalist perspective adapted three major ideas from biology; they are _____, _____, and _____.

8. In contrast to functionalist theory, conflict theory generally argues that _____, _____, and _____, or radical social change, are the major forces in society.

9. Symbolic interactionism argues that people act on the basis of their individual perceptions, not according to any _____.

10. Rational choice and learning theories were borrowed from other social sciences, the former from _____, the latter from _____.

11. Sociology in both English and French Canada can trace its origin to Park at the University of Chicago and the _____ approach, the study of communities.

12. S. D. Clark, along with _____, who studied the production of staples such as fur and cod, and McLuhan, who examined _____, were important in the development of sociology at _____.

13. From a functionalist perspective, the scarcity of Canadian sociology teachers in the 1960s can be seen as a _____, one correctable by the importing of American sociologists, thus returning the system to a state of _____ .

14. Francophone sociology, compared to its Anglophone counterpart, is today more applied and more _____ in its orientation and as a consequence less _____ .

15. The marginal value theorem is a part of _____ theory.

Answers

KEY TERMS AND DEFINITIONS

1. social facts
2. learning theory
3. functionalism
4. rational choice theory
5. symbolic interactionism
6. *verstehen*
7. conflict
8. dysfunction
9. equilibrium

SELF-QUIZ

1. c
2. e
3. b
4. a
5. d
6. d
7. c
8. c
9. d
10. d
11. b
12. e

FILL IN THE BLANKS

1. social facts
2. and what about the women
3. group membership, group, group
4. urbanized, heterogeneous
5. priests
6. understanding, predicting
7. function, equilibrium, development
8. power, disharmony, revolution
9. "objective" social reality
10. economics, psychology
11. human ecology
12. Innis, media and communication, University of Toronto
13. dysfunction, equilibrium
14. macro-sociological, quantitative
15. rational choice

CHAPTER 2

Research Methods

OBJECTIVES

1. To understand why sociologists conduct research and to appreciate the distinction between qualitative and quantitative methods.

2. To understand the workings of two major approaches — survey research and participant observation — on the following: theory, complexity of model, measurement, sampling, and data analysis, and to be able to compare and know the advantages and disadvantages of each.

3. To be aware of other specific research alternatives, like experiments and content analysis, as well as some general approaches to methods including Marxist and female-friendly science.

KEY TERMS AND DEFINITIONS

1. _____: a statistical demonstration that changes in one variable coincide with changes in another variable; not to be confused with cause.

2. _____: the actual procedures used to measure a theoretical concept, as in IQ scores being used to measure intelligence.

3. _____: the degree to which a measure actually measures what it claims to measure.

4. _____: a method that extracts themes from communications, including letters, books, and newspapers.

5. _____: records produced by contemporaries of an event.

6. _____: explanations that arise from the data and are thus based on reality rather than on deductive logic.

7. _____: Marx's concept that research should not be *pure*, conducted for knowledge's sake, but *applied*, undertaken to improve society.

8. _____: interpretations of primary sources made by others not immediately present at an event.

9. _____: the type of research that takes place at one point in time as opposed to _____ research which, because it takes place over a period of time, can detect change and better demonstrate cause.

10. _____: the derivation of a specific statement from a set of more general statements.

11. _____: a sample in which every member of the population is eligible for inclusion and individuals are selected by chance.

12. _____: the appearance that two variables are in a causal relationship, when in fact each is an effect of a common third variable.

13. _____: making connecting links between related statements for the purpose of deriving hypotheses.

14. _____: repeating a research project in an attempt to verify earlier findings.

15. _____: a series of random samples taken in units of decreasing size, such as census tracts, then streets, then houses, then residents.

16. _____: the degree to which repeated measurements of the same variable, using the same or equivalent instruments, are equal.

17. _____: variables included in a model of behaviour that are neither independent nor dependent variables. They are held constant to check on apparent relationships between independent and dependent variables.

18. _____: the group of subjects in an experiment that is exposed to the independent variable, as opposed to the _____ group which is not exposed.

19. _____: a set of interrelated statements or propositions about a particular subject matter.

20. _____: the generalizability of research results beyond the artificial laboratory experimental situation to the real world.

21. _____: a characteristic, such as income or religion, that takes on different values among different individuals or groups. Those that are causes are generally called _____ and those that are effects, _____.

22. _____: a research strategy wherein a researcher becomes a member of a group to study it and group members are aware that they are being observed.

23. _____: a statement of a presumed relationship between two or more variables.

24. _____: the construction of a generalization from a set of specific statements.

25. _____: the examination by a researcher of someone else's data.

26. _____: the systematic study of several cultures undertaken to compare them.

27. _____: the application of natural science research methods to social science.

28. _____: the application of several research methods to the same topic in the hope that the weaknesses of any one method may be compensated for by the strengths of others.

29. _____: a selection of people that matches the sample to the population on the basis of selected characteristics.

SELF-QUIZ

1. The research process should probably be described as
   a) funnel-like and circular
   b) linear
   c) triangular
   d) expanding
   e) logarithmic

2. Positivists would most likely use _____ in deriving their hypotheses.
   a) the construction of a generalization from a set of specific statements
   b) post-hoc explanations that arise from the data
   c) deductive logic
   d) connecting links between related statements
   e) first-person explanations of behaviour

3. Validity refers to
   a) those measures of a dependent variable taken before, not after, the introduction of an independent variable
   b) the degree to which repeated measurements of the same variable with the same instruments are equal
   c) a characteristic that takes on different values among different individuals
   d) consistency in longitudinal research
   e) none of the above

4. Which of the following statements is true?
   a) if a measure is not reliable, it cannot be valid
   b) if a measure is reliable, it is also valid
   c) generalizability is more important than validity
   d) b and c only
   e) a and c only

5. In the examination of the relationship between alcohol consumption and date rape among 19-year-old males, _____ is the independent variable.

   a) males
   b) gender
   c) age
   d) date rape
   e) alcohol consumption

6. If researchers want to generalize to the total population and do not have to worry about costs, which of the following would be the best type of sample to draw upon?

   a) systematic
   b) accidental
   c) quota
   d) random
   e) quasi-experimental

7. When examining tables, percentages allow more accurate comparisons than raw numbers. The only rule to remember about percentages is that

   a) each category of the dependent variable must add up to 100%
   b) each category of the independent variable must add up to 100%
   c) each category of the dependent variable must have equal cell sizes
   d) each category of the independent variable must have equal cell sizes
   e) b and d

8. Which research method attempts to keep the model quite simple by using random assignment and involving only the relevant independent and dependent variables?

   a) participant observation
   b) survey research
   c) content analysis
   d) experimental design
   e) ethnomethodology

9. Qualitative methods are marked by all of the following, except:

   a) humanism
   b) interpretation
   c) detachment
   d) value orientation
   e) b and d

10. Many participant observers refuse to derive hypotheses from theories, but instead use

    a) deductive logic
    b) grounded theory
    c) inductive logic
    d) a and b only
    e) b and c only

11. The issues of validity and generalizability are related and are at the heart of the debate between survey researchers and participant observers. Survey researchers argue that participant observation is inferior because
    a) of its difficulty in making generalizations
    b) of its operationalism
    c) it does not directly observe behaviour but elicits only verbal reports of that behaviour
    d) of its correlational nature
    e) c and d only

12. Female-friendly science would probably be most opposed to
    a) accepting personal experience
    b) positivism
    c) participant observation
    d) interdisciplinary approaches
    e) a breaking down of hierarchy

13. Which of the following is true of experimental designs?
    a) cause can be demonstrated more easily than in survey research or participant observation
    b) it is strong in both generalizability and validity
    c) studies are easily replicable
    d) a and b only
    e) a and c only

14. Which method is least likely to be replicated?
    a) the experiment
    b) participant observation
    c) survey research
    d) content analysis
    e) random digit dialing

15. Content analysis is a less-frequently used research method of sociology and involves extracting themes from communications. Among its major strengths is the fact that
    a) it is inexpensive
    b) it is strong on validity
    c) it does not allow researchers to intrude upon the data
    d) causal relationships can be demonstrated easily
    e) a and c only

FILL IN THE BLANKS

1. A list of all possible individual units in a population is called a _____.

2. In the statement, "As integration varies, suicide rates vary," integration is the _____ variable and suicide rates the _____ variable.

3. Hypothesizing that, since religious students are less deviant they will also be less likely to seek abortions, is an example of _____ logic.

4. A _____ approach, which sees history as a series of conflicts over existing material arrangements, is attractive to Marxists. It maintains that the seeds for transformation exist in every society, with the new society containing seeds for its own transformation.

5. Whether crime should be measured by arrest rates, conviction rates, or victim surveys raises the issue of _____.

6. To examine whether the colour of the packaging influences ice cream sales for men and women separately would make gender the _____ variable.

7. You do not need a phone book if you draw your sample using _____.

8. There are only two rules of sampling; first, a sample should be _____ of the population from which it is drawn and, second, conclusions should not be _____ beyond the groups from which the sample is drawn.

9. As a general rule, when analyzing data tables you should avoid examining actual numbers. _____ allow more accurate comparisons to be made.

10. Qualitative data are not objective data for all that is known about the social world is a consequence of _____.

11. In the most simple social science experiment, there are two groups of subjects, the experimental and the control group. In a study of the effectiveness of a new drug, the _____ group would get the placebo, or sugar pill.

12. A crucial difference between survey research and experiments is that the effects of all other variables not included in experimental models are supposed to be eliminated through the _____ of subjects to groups.

13. Perspective rather than theory, subjectivity, and a complex picture of a small number of cases mean we are probably describing _____.

14. Noting that Bill, John, Nick, and other boys are more aggressive than Mary, Liz, Joan, and other girls, and then concluding that boys are more aggressive than girls, is an example of _____ theory.

15. In their disputes with survey researchers, participant observers, while admitting to limited generalizability due to their small samples, lay claim to greater _____ because they observe _____.

16. Standpoint and the biographical method are types of _____ research.

17. Comparing experiments, survey research, and participant observation, validity is potentially strongest in _____. For generalizability, _____ may be best and the other two methods weaker. Finally, concerning cause, _____ excel and survey research is weaker.

18. Empathy and understanding are more characteristic of qualitative or quantitative methods? _____.

19. Because of their interest in social change, Marxists are more likely than functionalists to pay attention to _____ in their analysis.

20. Merely being in an experiment can alter people's behaviour as they try to please the experimenter. This is called the _____.

Answers

KEY TERMS AND DEFINITIONS

1. correlation
2. operational definition
3. validity
4. content analysis
5. primary sources
6. grounded theory
7. praxis
8. secondary sources
9. cross-sectional, longitudinal
10. deductive logic
11. random sample
12. spurious relationship
13. axiomatic logic
14. replication
15. cluster sampling
16. reliability
17. control variables
18. experimental, control
19. theory
20. external validity
21. variable, independent, dependent
22. participant observation
23. hypothesis
24. inductive logic
25. secondary analysis
26. comparative analysis
27. positivism
28. triangulation
29. quota sample

SELF-QUIZ

1. a
2. c
3. e
4. a
5. e
6. d
7. b
8. d
9. c
10. e
11. a
12. b
13. e
14. b
15. e

FILL IN THE BLANKS

1. sampling frame
2. independent, dependent
3. deductive
4. dialectical
5. validity
6. control
7. random-digit dialing
8. representative, generalized
9. Percentages
10. interpretation
11. control
12. random assignment
13. participant observation
14. grounded
15. validity, actual behaviour
16. qualitative
17. participant observation, survey research, experiments
18. qualitative
19. history
20. Hawthorne effect

CHAPTER 3

Culture

OBJECTIVES

1. To define culture and to distinguish and understand its major sociological aspects.

2. To be aware of the existence of cultural variation and of arguments concerning cultural differences between the United States and Canada.

3. To appreciate cultural integration, the scarcity of cultural universals, and the errors of ethnocentrism, especially its Eurocentric and androcentric variants.

4. To understand four major theoretical perspectives used to explain cultural variation: functionalism, conflict theory, cultural materialism, and feminism, and to be introduced to cultural studies.

KEY TERMS AND DEFINITIONS

1. _____ : the sum total of all cultural elements associated with a given social group.

2. _____ : a specific set of norms and values that the members of a society use to regulate some broad area of social life.

3. _____ : those norms that when violated provoke a relatively strong reaction on the part of other group members.

4. _____ : a subset of individuals within a society who are characterized by certain cultural elements that set them apart from others in the society.

5. _____ : a group of people who reside in the same geographical area, who communicate extensively among themselves, and who share a common culture.

6. _____ : anything that (1) is shared in common by the members of some social group; (2) is passed on to new members; and (3) in some way affects their behaviour or perceptions of the world. Three of the most important are values, norms, and roles.

7. _____ : relatively general beliefs that define right and wrong, or that indicate general preferences.

8. _____: applied to culture, the theoretical perspective that explains cultural elements by showing how they contribute to societal stability.

9. _____: elements of culture found in all known societies.

10. _____: seeing things from the perspective of one's own culture. It includes the belief that one's own culture is superior to others and the belief that what is true of one's culture is true of others.

11. _____: stories of the recent past, told orally, which although believed to be true, are actually false and reflect unconscious fears.

12. _____: relatively precise rules specifying the behaviours permitted and those that are prohibited for group members.

13. _____: all the physical objects manufactured or used by the members of a society or a subculture.

14. _____: those norms that when violated do not provoke a strong reaction on the part of other group members.

15. _____: a cluster of behavioural expectations associated with some particular social position within a group or society.

16. _____: the interrelationship of elements in a given culture such that a change in one element can lead to changes, sometimes unexpected, in other elements.

17. _____: those preferences and objects that are widely distributed across all social classes in a society.

18. _____: a theoretical perspective in which cultural elements are explained by showing how they are pragmatic and rational adaptations to the material environment.

19. _____: a situation in which the behavioural expectations of one role are inconsistent with those of another concurrent role.

SELF-QUIZ

1. The insert about the Nuer and the father role could be used to illustrate the issue of
   a) folkways versus mores
   b) cultural universals, in this case that fathers generally must be males
   c) avunculate
   d) urban legends
   e) structuralism

2. If people simultaneously try to be parents of young children and full-time workers, they may experience

   a) status enhancement
   b) role conflict
   c) cultural integration
   d) anomic suicidal tendencies
   e) egoistic suicidal tendencies

3. Nymphomania should be coupled with

   a) AIDS
   b) folkways
   c) mores
   d) structuralism but not functionalism
   e) satyriasis

4. The major distinction between folkways and mores is

   a) in the nature of the reaction that a violation of the norm produces and not in the content of the rule
   b) in the content of the rule and not in the nature of the reaction that a violation of the norm produces
   c) in the nature of the reaction that a violation of the norm produces and in the content of the rule
   d) in neither the reaction nor the content
   e) this question cannot be answered without more information

5. Which of the following most likely involves a violation of a folkway?

   a) childless couples
   b) income tax evasion
   c) having three spouses at the same time
   d) fatalistic suicide
   e) egoistic suicide

6. According to a conflict interpretation, Mother Theresa can be criticized for

   a) being too good and scaring others
   b) not helping enough in her native Yugoslavia
   c) deflecting attention from the real issue of inequality
   d) a and b
   e) a and c

7. Which of the following is false?

   a) most laws are social norms
   b) most social norms are laws
   c) many norms that structure behaviour are implicit
   d) a and c
   e) b and c

8. Barbie reinforces stereotypical female traits except with respect to
    a) being a wife and mother
    b) being well dressed
    c) being heterosexual
    d) her occupation
    e) being a consumer

9. Which of the following groups living in Canada could not constitute a subculture?
    a) Jews
    b) Italians
    c) Iranians
    d) Inuit
    e) a through d are all subcultures

10. Investigators of culture have consistently found that
    a) cultures exhibit enormous variation with regard to the content of their values, norms, and roles
    b) the elements of culture in a given society are often interrelated
    c) only a few cultural elements are common to all known societies
    d) a and b
    e) a, b, and c

11. According to Lipset, which of the following factors did not contribute to Canada's greater emphasis (in comparison to the American emphasis) on group harmony?
    a) Canada's strong ties to the British monarchy
    b) the U.S. and Canada's similar frontier experiences
    c) the dominant religion in English Canada being Anglican
    d) all of the above
    e) none of the above

12. Which of the following can be classified as an object of popular culture?
    a) a television set
    b) a collection of Mozart's work
    c) a Kentucky Fried Chicken franchise
    d) an antique automobile
    e) a and c only

13. Lipstick messages on mirrors welcoming men to the world of AIDS were used to illustrate
    a) urban legends
    b) popular culture
    c) cultural materialism
    d) American versus Canadian value differences
    e) mores

14. Which perspective would explain a norm by showing how it contributes to the survival of the society in which it is found?

   a) cultural materialism
   b) functionalism
   c) conflict sociology
   d) symbolic interactionism
   e) feminism

15. Berdache is most closely associated with

   a) religious sacrificial rites
   b) fishing
   c) the Arapesh
   d) androcentricism
   e) being two-spirited

FILL IN THE BLANKS

1. The elements of culture that sociologists consider to be most important are _____, _____, and _____.

2. A ban on the eating of pork was used to illustrate the discussion of _____.

3. The belief that all societies should have a leader or chief and a discussion of prehistoric Venuses were used to illustrate _____.

4. The discussion of the wet-nurse was used to show that the _____, as we understand it, is not universal.

5. The use of the term "hunting and gathering societies," rather than "gathering and hunting societies," can be used to illustrate the variety of ethnocentrism called _____.

6. Margaret Mead (1935) discovered cultural variation in the area of sex roles. In the Mundugamor society, both males and females were expected to be _____. Among the Arapesh, both sexes were expected to be _____. Among the Tchambuli, _____ was associated with females and _____ with males.

7. Most social anthropologists during the nineteenth century believed that societies pass through three stages labelled _____, _____, and _____. Such ideas are an example of _____.

8. _____ is an interdisciplinary approach to the study of culture, one that is increasingly popular among sociologists.

9. The disintegration of the Yir Yoront culture is an extreme example of the importance of _____.

10. Malinowski's explanation of the Trobrianders' use of magic in their ocean fishing uses the _____ perspective.

Answers

KEY TERMS AND DEFINITIONS

1. culture
2. institution
3. mores
4. subculture
5. society
6. cultural element
7. values
8. functionalism
9. cultural universals
10. ethnocentrism
11. urban legends
12. norms
13. material culture
14. folkways
15. role
16. cultural integration
17. popular culture
18. cultural materialism
19. role conflict

SELF-QUIZ

1. b
2. b
3. e
4. a
5. a
6. c
7. b
8. a
9. e
10. e
11. b
12. a
13. a
14. b
15. e

FILL IN THE BLANKS

1. values, norms, roles
2. cultural materialism
3. Eurocentrism
4. mother role
5. androcentrism
6. aggressive, passive, aggression, passivity
7. savagery, barbarism, civilization, ethnocentrism
8. Cultural studies
9. cultural integration
10. functionalist

CHAPTER 4

Socialization

OBJECTIVES

1. Using a variety of perspectives to define socialization and appreciate the contents and limits of the nature versus nurture debate.

2. To be aware of functionalist, conflict, and symbolic interactionist perspectives on socialization.

3. To understand three psychological approaches to socialization: psychodynamic, cognitive, and social learning, as well as briefly describe the contributions of major theorists found within each theoretical framework.

4. To be aware of the various agents and contexts and how they have changed over the past 200 years.

KEY TERMS AND DEFINITIONS

1. _____: the means by which someone is made "fit" to live among other humans.

2. _____: the ways in which societies reproduce themselves in terms of privilege and status.

3. _____: the stage of moral development in which children believe that ethical rules are absolute, coming from some higher external authority.

4. _____: Cooley's idea that personality is shaped when individuals see themselves mirrored in the reactions of others.

5. _____: Mead's term for individuals' attempts to put themselves in others' shoes to imagine what the others are thinking, thus enabling them to see themselves as others see them.

6. _____: the stages through which individuals pass as they grow and mature from an embryo through adulthood.

7. _____: the learning of the attitudes, beliefs, and behaviours related to roles individuals expect to play in the future.

8. _____: the major components of Freud's model of personality. The _____ is that unconscious aspect of personality that is impulsive and pleasure-seeking. The _____ includes intellectual and cognitive processes. Most of it is conscious and guided by the reality principle: ideas and actions are modified to fit actual experiences. The _____ consists largely of what is generally called "conscience."

9. _____: socialization attempts that have unintended consequences.

10. _____: persons whose attitudes and opinions affect one's life. They include family and friends as well as people of high prestige like teachers and celebrities.

11. _____: the debate over the extent to which human behaviour is affected by genetic versus social factors.

12. _____: that which occurs when a person is not exposed to all of the experiences necessary to function in certain roles.

13. _____: the stage of moral development in which children see rules as products of negotiation and agreement rather than as absolute. At the stage of _____, individuals can operate and think independently of authority, rules, and laws.

14. _____: the term in human development theory, comparing a person to a flower, with preset stages of growth, the outcome of which is determined by how well or poorly the environment nurtures it during that stage.

15. _____: socialization processes that lack continuity between contexts, making it difficult for people to make transitions to or adjust to new contexts.

16. _____: the individual's conception of what is expected, of normative behaviour; it provides a unified basis for self-reference.

17. _____: an interrelated set of social positions in which people share common expectations about desired outcomes as part of a division of labour.

18. _____: the two aspects of Mead's conception of the self. The first is the impulsive, creative aspect; the second is more deliberative and cautious than the first.

19. _____: the number of socializers versus those being socialized. The lower the figure, the less the context will change those being socialized.

20. _____: those cultures in which relations between parents and offspring are governed by traditional norms beyond questioning of either generation. Contrast this to _____, in which social changes makes the intergenerational linkage tenuous, and _____, in which social change is so great that parental life experiences are so dated that parental guidance is not well regarded by children.

21. _____: the first stage in Piaget's theory representing the infant's concern with understanding how needs can be met by the external environment. The second or _____ stage involves the early use of concept formation and intuition by children. The third or _____ stage describes how people learn basic logic and social perspective taking. The last or _____ stage occurs when people have the ability to use propositional thinking and abstract reasoning in a variety of contexts. It is a role-taking stage.

SELF-QUIZ

1. One function of socialization includes
   a) development of an individual's personality
   b) equality
   c) cultural transmission
   d) developing the "I"
   e) a and c

2. Defining dating as a rehearsal for playing marital roles illustrates the concept of
   a) resocialization
   b) anticipatory socialization
   c) fixation
   d) modelling
   e) vicarious punishment

3. The phallic or last stage identified by Freud would most likely come at the _____ stage identified by Piaget.
   a) moral realism
   b) morality of cooperation
   c) morality of constraints
   d) cognitive
   e) a and b

4. Which is not one of Erikson's opposites?

   a) intimacy/isolation
   b) industry/inferiority
   c) growth/death
   d) trust/distrust
   e) initiative/guilt

5. The psychodynamic perspective focuses on

   a) the perceptions individuals have of their interactions with others
   b) the development of individuals as members of various groups
   c) the development of various internal characteristics and processes
   d) social learning processes
   e) vicarious punishment and reinforcement

6. Of Freud's three major components of personality, the one most likely to make you ignore others and take care of yourself is the

   a) id
   b) reality principle
   c) superego
   d) maternal instinct
   e) ego

7. In reference to Erikson's theory of development, in adolescence individuals develop

   a) trust
   b) autonomy
   c) initiative
   d) industry
   e) a sense of identity

8. Which theory argues that individuals constantly have a view or sense of themselves that is defined and affected by the actions and reactions of other people toward them?

   a) Erikson's "psychological" theory
   b) Freud's personality development theory
   c) symbolic interactionism
   d) modelling theory
   e) none of the above

9. The development of the self takes place in two stages according to Mead. Which of the following is part of Mead's theory?

   a) the play stage
   b) the latency stage
   c) the symbolic stage
   d) the looking-glass self stage
   e) the reality stage

10. Socialization includes all of the following, except:

   a) pressuring
   b) government control
   c) learning
   d) conditioning
   e) a and d

11. The _____ socialization context has diminished in importance while the _____ context has increased over the last two centuries.

   a) peers, media
   b) peers, religion
   c) family, peers
   d) religion, family
   e) education, peers

12. According to Bettelheim, most feral children are probably

   a) retarded
   b) fetal alcohol syndrome victims
   c) prefigurative
   d) postfigurative
   e) autistic

13. While in the 1980s students wanted to be well off financially, in the 1960s they wanted to

   a) support civil rights
   b) engage in sex
   c) develop a meaningful philosophy of life
   d) maximize their nature
   e) a and b

14. Television and surfing the net take time away from other activities. This is called the _____ effect.

   a) displacement
   b) surrogacy
   c) vicarious
   d) content interchange
   e) teenzine

15. There is no _____ but rather a multitude of human needs, potential, and limitations found in all of us.

   a) agency
   b) conscience
   c) feral childhood
   d) one function of socialization
   e) one human nature

16. The first of Piaget's cognitive development stages is
    a) formal operations
    b) pre-operations
    c) concrete operations
    d) moral autonomy
    e) sensorimotor

17. Ego identity is also called _____ continuity.
    a) self-other
    b) other-self
    c) self-self
    d) negative
    e) positive

18. Margaret Mead was especially interested in the idea that adolescence is inevitably a time of
    a) cultural relativity
    b) latency
    c) storm and stress
    d) game stage
    e) moral realism

19. *Coming of Age in Samoa* was written by
    a) Margaret Mead
    b) Benedict
    c) Erikson
    d) G.H. Mead
    e) Cooley

20. The keg that set the stage for Littleton was
    a) adolescent storm and stress
    b) sexual needs
    c) cliques
    d) the decline of religion
    e) mass media violence

FILL IN THE BLANKS

1. We can see the significance of socialization by comparing normal children with those raised in non-human environments. These children are often labelled feral because they act like _____.

2. The controversial _____ movement sought to perfect the human gene pool.

28 Introduction to Sociology Study Guide

3. Erikson identified _____ stages of ego development, from developing trust in infancy to evaluating one's life in old age.

4. Finding that adopted children are more similar to their biological parents (from whom they have been separated) than to their adoptive parents would provide evidence for _____ contributions to personality development.

5. In the _____ stage, children develop more unified conceptions of themselves as they simultaneously learn to take the role of others.

6. Very young children believe in a morality of _____.

7. The ego's interactions with the world are guided by the _____ .

8. Prisoners often have to replace old roles and thoughts with new ones in order to become "good prisoners." This is an example of _____.

9. Disagreements regarding how much free will people have in their dealings with social structure is more broadly known as the _____ debate.

10. The _____ (Thomas, 1923) refers to the thought processes people use to interpret their environments. They may then act on these interpretations.

11. Strictly speaking, while puberty is a biological phenomenon, _____ is cultural phenomenon.

12. The _____ is marked by behavioural disarray and a lack of a recognized role in the community.

13. Psychologists are interested in _____ people learn, sociologists in _____ people learn.

14. _____ try to show how behaviour patterns are affected by natural selection.

15. Freud's theory of personality development falls under the _____ theoretical perspective, which focuses on the development of various internal characteristics and processes.

16. The mature personality develops through several stages, according to Freud. They are as follows: first is the _____ stage; second the _____ stage; third the _____ stage; fourth the _____ stage; and last the _____ stage.

17. Viewing individuals as not having the agency to resist social pressures is called the _____.

18. Tolerance that arises from reduced ethnocentrism is called cultural _____.

19. If at the end of a boring lecture you refrain from telling your teacher this view, the _____ aspect of the self is controlling your behaviour (Mead's term).

20. On Valentine's day you might send a card to your _____ other.

Answers

KEY TERMS AND DEFINITIONS

1. socialization
2. social reproduction
3. morality of constraints
4. looking-glass self
5. role taking
6. ontogenetic stages
7. anticipatory socialization
8. id, ego, superego
9. defective socialization
10. significant others
11. nature versus nurture
12. inadequate socialization
13. morality of cooperation, moral autonomy
14. epigenetic
15. disjunctive socialization
16. generalized other
17. role system
18. "I," "me"
19. socialization ratio
20. postfigurative, cofigurative, prefigurative cultures
21. sensorimotor, pre-operational, concrete operational, formal operational stages

SELF-QUIZ

1. e
2. b
3. b
4. c
5. c
6. a
7. c
8. c
9. a
10. b
11. c
12. e
13. c
14. a
15. e
16. e
17. c
18. c
19. a
20. c

FILL IN THE BLANKS

1. animals
2. eugenics
3. eight
4. genetic
5. game
6. constraints
7. reality principle
8. resocialization
9. structure-agency
10. definition of the situation
11. adolescence
12. identity crisis
13. how, what
14. Sociobiologists
15. psychodynamic
16. oral, anal, phallic, latency, genital
17. oversocialized conception of humanity
18. relativity
19. me
20. significant

CHAPTER 5

Deviance

OBJECTIVES

1. To understand what is meant by deviance and how societies decide what is deviant and what is not. The latter will include functionalist, conflict, and other explanations.

2. To understand how deviance is counted and the need for an audience reaction for deviance to exist.

3. To be familiar with social structural explanations of deviance and their limitations.

4. To be aware of the strengths and weaknesses of social process theories of deviance.

KEY TERMS AND DEFINITIONS

1. _____: the explanation that views the widespread discrepancy between a society's goals and the legitimate means it provides to achieve those goals as leading to normlessness and eventually to deviance.

2. _____: the view that the economic elite is the single major force behind definitions of what is and what is not deviant.

3. _____: body types (thin, fat, and muscular respectively) tested for their relationship to personality and then to crime and delinquency.

4. _____: the explanation of deviance which argues that societal reactions to minor deviance may alienate those so stigmatized and may cut off their options for conformity, thus leading to greater deviance as an adaptation to the stigma.

5. _____: Merton's four deviant adaptations to the problems created when society provides insufficient means to achieve its goals are: _____, who find illegitimate means, _____, who water down goals, _____, who give up goals and means, and _____ who seek both new goals and new means.

6. _____: wrongdoing that is engaged in by a large part of the population and generally tolerated, for example, exceeding the speed limit.

7. _____: a theory that sees deviance as learned in small-group interaction, wherein an individual internalizes an excess of pro-deviant perspectives.

8. _____: the process through which the actual number of crimes committed is reduced due to fear or reporting, bias, discretion, or human error.

9. _____: the deviance which arises out of anger, alienation, limiting of options, and change of self concept that may occur after a negative social reaction or labelling.

10. _____: a group of individuals who share a similar trait defined as deviant by the larger society that for them is normal and important to their identity.

11. _____: those who commit deviant acts but to whom no one responds as if they have done so, either because they are not caught, or, if caught, because they are excused for some reason.

12. _____: Durkheim's term for the set of agreed-upon standards of society assumed to have arisen from consensus.

13. _____: people who seek to influence the making of rules and definitions of deviance.

14. _____: an argument stating that punishing individuals for minor forms of deviance may backfire and encourage them to take up deviant careers.

15. _____: the view that power is shared and that definitions of deviance arise not from consensus, nor from any one group, but from a diversity of sources.

16. _____: a way of life in opposition to, as opposed to merely distinct from, the larger culture.

17. _____: Cohen's name for the tendency of working class delinquents to invert middle class values as a form of protest.

18. _____: rationalizations that allow deviants to define their behaviour as acceptable.

19. _____: conditions or behaviour perceived by society as not normal and at least somewhat disvalued and thus an acceptable target for social control.

SELF-QUIZ

1. In arguing that stores can afford a bit of shoplifting, a thief is using which technique of neutralization?

    a) denial of personal responsibility
    b) denial of injury
    c) condemning the condemners
    d) denial of the victim
    e) appeal to higher loyalties

2. Commitment, beliefs, involvement, and attachment should remind you of _____ theory.

    a) social control
    b) anomie
    c) labelling
    d) psychological
    e) critical

3. According to functionalists, definitions of deviance come from

    a) moral entrepreneurs
    b) the collective conscience
    c) false consciousness
    d) the proletariat (working class)
    e) the economic elite

4. Which of the following groups does not exceed its opposites in mental illness rates?

    a) the young
    b) males
    c) urban areas
    d) the poor
    e) the divorced

5. Sheldon sought explanations for crime in biology and hypothesized that biological variables, especially body type, lead to personality variables which in turn lead to crime. He argued that _____ are more likely to commit crimes.

    a) ectomorphs
    b) mesomorphs
    c) endomorphs
    d) individuals with XYY chromosomes
    e) none of the above, all body types are equal in their criminality

6. Biological explanations of deviance are criticized for

    a) often ignoring women
    b) being atavistic
    c) being unable to account for fluctuations over time of deviance rates
    d) b and c
    e) a and c

7. Arguing that you learned to shoplift because your friends taught you that such behaviour is acceptable would be consistent with _____ theory.

   a) anomie
   b) differential association
   c) labelling
   d) deviance amplification
   e) relative deprivation

8. According to Smith, which of the following (is) are not (a) correlate(s) of the physical forms of wife abuse?

   a) unemployment of husband
   b) low family income
   c) low educational achievement of husband
   d) low educational achievement of wife
   e) ethnicity and religious affiliation

9. Although Merton's theory of anomie is flawed, its greatest contribution to the study of deviance is its argument

   a) that social factors are important in explaining individual deviance
   b) that deviance is caused by biological, psychological, *and* social factors
   c) that deviance does not exist without a reaction
   d) that calling attention to minor deviance may encourage major deviance
   e) none of the above

10. Which of the following is not a major point of the labelling perspective?

    a) individuals are neither totally deviant nor totally conformist but instead possess aspects of both
    b) labelling and punishing individuals may lead to more and not less deviance
    c) deviance is learned, usually alone, but sometimes with others
    d) an individual may become the victim of role engulfment
    e) part of the anger among those labelled concerns the existence of rule-breakers

11. Looking at the crimes of the powerful would most likely be the concern of a(n) _____ theorist.

    a) anomie
    b) differential association
    c) functionalist
    d) radical
    e) psychological

12. Arguments against collecting crime statistics by race and ethnic categories did not include

    a) difficulties in measuring race and ethnicity
    b) the need to examine social class factors
    c) the fact that some types of crimes do not get full police attention
    d) the fact that deviance needs a reaction as well as an action
    e) a and b

13. Labelling theorists can be placed into the larger theoretical perspective of _____ since they argue that the deviant's definitions of self and of the situation are crucial.

   a) social structure
   b) conflict theory
   c) symbolic interactionism
   d) functionalism
   e) pluralism

14. Which of the following individuals is more likely to commit a crime?

   a) a young female in Prince Edward Island from a disadvantaged background
   b) an older male in an urban area in British Columbia
   c) a young male in New Brunswick with a grade 12 education
   d) a young female in a rural area with a grade 8 education
   e) a young male in Alberta with a grade 6 education

15. According to functionalism, deviance can benefit society in which of the following ways?

   a) deviance may begin a process of adaptation and progress to new and better norms and values
   b) deviance may aid in the process of greater social equality
   c) deviance helps unify the different layers of society since almost everyone commits a deviant act at one time or another
   d) a and c only
   e) b and c only

FILL IN THE BLANKS

1. The different definitions of deviance found among the Inuit society compared with the rest of Canada illustrate the relative definition of deviance, that what is deviant is specific to _____, _____, and _____.

2. Halloween, smoke detectors, and marking the bottom layer of society were each mentioned in the discussion of _____.

3. The process whereby an individual's deviance becomes a master status is called _____. Good traits are ignored or misinterpreted, while bad ones are magnified out of proportion.

4. The deviance committed before any social reaction and arising from a variety of causes is called _____.

5. Freudians might see mental illness as due to the inability of the _____ to handle conflicts among the id, the superego, and the external world.

36   Introduction to Sociology Study Guide

6. Widespread fluctuations this century in crime, alcoholism, and mental illness rates cast doubt on _____ explanations of deviance.

7. Merton argued that the discrepancy between the goals a society instills and the acceptable means the society provides to achieve the goals can lead to a state of _____, a large-scale breakdown of rules which he called _____.

8. Working class people who live in modest homes, have older cars, and take few vacations are called _____, according to Merton's scheme.

9. Applied by society to those whom it considers deviant, _____ redefines their past behaviour as deviant as well.

10. At the bottom of the crime funnel are _____, taken from court records.

11. In general the _____ may be more frequently labelled for minor acts of crime and delinquency than the _____, but for serious forms this bias may be less important.

12. Some criminologists accept the argument of _____, that those who suffer crime may play a part in the process, making them the specific targets of criminals.

13. Cohen's delinquent boys, according to the text, are closest to Merton's _____.

14. The need for a reaction as well as an action for deviance led to a discussion of _____ versus _____, the former being those not caught for their deviance, the latter being those caught.

15. A focus on the coming together in time and space of victims, criminals, and a lack of social control is the main point of the _____ explanation of crime.

Answers

KEY TERMS AND DEFINITIONS

1. anomie
2. critical school
3. ectomorphs, endomorphs, mesomorphs
4. labelling theory
5. innovators, ritualists, retreatists, rebels
6. acceptable deviance
7. differential association
8. crime funnel
9. secondary deviance
10. deviant subculture
11. rule-breakers
12. collective conscience
13. moral entrepreneurs
14. deviance amplifying process
15. pluralism
16. counterculture
17. reaction formation
18. techniques of neutralization
19. deviance

SELF-QUIZ

1. b
2. a
3. b
4. a
5. b
6. e
7. b
8. e
9. a
10. c
11. d
12. b
13. c
14. e
15. a

FILL IN THE BLANKS

1. time, place, circumstance
2. the functions of deviance
3. role engulfment
4. primary deviance
5. ego
6. biological
7. normlessness, anomie
8. ritualists
9. retrospective interpretation
10. convictions
11. powerless, powerful
12. victim precipitation
13. rebels
14. rule breakers, deviants
15. routine activities approach

CHAPTER 6

Social Stratification

OBJECTIVES

1. To understand the basic concepts and definitions involved in the study of social stratification: status, stratum, status hierarchies and power dimensions, ascribed and achieved status, social mobility, class, and social class.

2. To understand several of the major theories of social stratification, including Marxist, Weberian, and structural-functionalist positions.

3. To be aware of Canada's stratification structure, including the eight most important factors of social differentiation and their interrelationships: wealth and property, occupation, education, race/ethnicity, region and rural-urban location, gender, age, and political power.

4. To be aware of some of the major consequences of stratification for people, including its effects on life chances, life-styles, values, and beliefs.

KEY TERMS AND DEFINITIONS

1. _____: a set of individuals sharing a similar economic status or market position.

2. _____: Marx's word for the working class, the non-owners of the means of production.

3. _____: the combination of statuses that any one individual occupies.

4. _____: Weber's three (as opposed to Marx's one) bases of _____ social inequality.

5. _____: movement or change between parental status and a child's status in the same status hierarchy.

6. _____: movement up and down a status hierarchy.

7. _____: a position in a status hierarchy which is attained by individual effort or accomplishment.

8. _____: a Marxian category including people who share the same economic position but who may be unaware of their common class position.

Chapter 6: Social Stratification 39

9. _____: the tendency for diversification and complexity in the statuses and characteristics of social life.

10. _____: any one of a set of rankings along which statuses are rated in terms of their power.

11. _____: movement by an individual from one status to another of similar rank within the same status hierarchy.

12. _____: any position occupied by an individual in a social system.

13. _____: a set of statuses of similar rank in any status hierarchy.

14. _____: the capitalist class, as defined by Marx. The _____ were the small-property owners, a group he predicted would be swallowed by the larger capitalists.

15. _____: sometimes called domination, it becomes a regular part of everyday human existence, usually because it is established in formal laws or accepted customs.

16. _____: dissimilarity in the rankings of an individual's statuses in a set of status hierarchies.

17. _____: a position in a status hierarchy that is inherited or assigned.

18. _____: movement by an individual from one status to another in the same status hierarchy during a lifetime or career.

19. _____: similarity in the rankings of an individual's statuses in a set of status hierarchies.

20. _____: a Marxian category including people who share the same economic position, are aware of their common class position, and who thus may become agents for social change.

21. _____: a category of individuals who possess similar economic position as well as group consciousness, common identity, and a tendency to act as a social unit.

22. _____: the general pattern of inequality or ranking of socially differentiated characteristics.

23. _____: a differential capacity to command resources and thereby control social situations.

SELF-QUIZ

1. It has been argued that the study of social stratification is concerned mainly with "who gets what and why." In this view social stratification is

    a) independent of power
    b) a distributive process
    c) an example of capitalism in its purest form
    d) concerned with class for itself not class in itself
    e) a study of the micro-elements in society

2. Concerning status consistency, which is true?

    a) it probably relates more to wealth than to occupation
    b) status consistency is almost never found
    c) a high degree of status consistency tends to indicate a "closed" stratification system
    d) it relates mainly to ascribed statuses
    e) it relates mainly to achieved statuses

3. Which of the following is (are) (an) ascribed status?

    a) educational status
    b) ethnic origin
    c) occupational status
    d) a and b
    e) a, b, and c

4. Power that arises largely from control over human resources or the activities of other people is _____ power.

    a) economic
    b) political
    c) ideological
    d) institutionalized
    e) domination

5. For Marx, apart from obvious differences in wealth and prestige, what really underlies the division of societies into two opposing groups is

    a) the power that derives from ownership or non-ownership of property
    b) the proletariat and the bourgeoisie
    c) the structure and the superstructure
    d) class for itself and class in itself
    e) none of the above

6. Marx did not advocate

    a) equal liability of all to labour
    b) centralization of credit
    c) a graduated income tax
    d) the continued distinction between town and country
    e) free education

7. Weber's concept of power in social organizational theory can best be labelled

    a) conflict
    b) functional
    c) pluralist
    d) symbolic interactionist
    e) positivist

8. Attaching greater rewards to those positions either deemed crucial or requiring rare skills than to less valuable ones is a part of which perspective?

    a) structural-functionalism
    b) symbolic interactionism
    c) pluralism
    d) conflict
    e) none of the above

9. In societies such as Canada, in which wealth and property can be inherited, there is a tendency toward reduced

    a) horizontal mobility
    b) status consistency
    c) vertical social mobility
    d) generational conflict
    e) class structure

10. Which of the following is true concerning Canada's income distribution?

    a) income is more widely diffused in the population today than ever before
    b) the distribution of wealth has not changed very much in recent decades
    c) government programs to redistribute income from the very rich to the lower strata have generally been successful
    d) the upper strata received relatively less income in the 1990s than in the 1950s
    e) c and d

11. The best single indicator of an individual's general stratum position is

    a) income
    b) education
    c) ethnicity
    d) sex
    e) occupation

12. Which of the following statements is true?

    a) equal opportunity exists for all Canadians to acquire education
    b) in Canada today, ascriptive traits are still related to educational achievement, although perhaps less so than historically
    c) inequality of access has little to do with the differences in education levels among the population
    d) Canada's universal access to education has guaranteed an open stratification system
    e) a and d only

13. According to Porter, Canada resembles a "vertical mosaic," a social structure
    a) marked by a high degree of status consistency
    b) in which wealth and property can be passed on through inheritance
    c) in which the distribution of wealth is increasingly more widely diffused among various racial and ethnic groups
    d) comprising many diverse racial and ethnic groups, ranked along a hierarchy of power and privilege
    e) in which enormous variation exists in the ranking of various norms and values

14. The "new working class" is comprised of
    a) technical computer workers
    b) semi-skilled members of the working class
    c) pink-collar ghetto workers
    d) the *lumpenproletariat*
    e) contract workers

15. Which of the following is not a characteristic of a metropolis as opposed to a hinterland?
    a) seat of political power
    b) large-scale industry
    c) large universities
    d) source of raw materials
    e) population centre

16. Which of the following is false?
    a) women made up over 45% of the labour force in 1996
    b) among full-time employees, women make only 73% of the average male wage
    c) women's lower pay is largely a function of their lesser training and experience
    d) the female disadvantage in pay is more evident among older cohorts
    e) a through d are false

17. It would appear that political power is associated with the other sources of power that determine the distribution of wealth, prestige, and other resources in this country. Those who tend to dominate are
    a) of foreign origin and live outside Canada
    b) male and of French origin
    c) the economic elites who live in hinterland areas
    d) central Canadians, of British origin, and male
    e) central Canadians and of French origin

18. Which of the following statements is true in reference to social stratification?
    a) those with more to spend are more likely to place a greater emphasis on home life than those from the lower strata
    b) lower-class individuals are more susceptible to a broad spectrum of physical and mental illnesses than their more prosperous counterparts
    c) the working class tends to place less value than its counterparts on material success and financial security
    d) daily life in the upper strata is characterized by greater restrictiveness than life in the lower strata
    e) a and b

FILL IN THE BLANKS

1. _____ is the financial capital of the nation.

2. Evidence indicates that the top 10 percent of the Canadian population holds over _____ of all wealth. Both stocks and dividends are disproportionately theirs.

3. According to Marx, history is a series of struggles between haves and have-nots, today capitalist and worker, previously _____ and _____, and before that _____ and _____.

4. Most researchers suggest that age has an up-and-down, or _____, association with stratification.

5. We usually discuss _____ mobility as most indicative of an open stratification system.

6. If, as a group, manual labourers were to have similar economic power, they would constitute a _____.

7. Probably the greatest wealth is found in the province of _____, while the least is found in the _____ provinces.

8. Marx focused on private ownership of productive property, or what he called the _____.

9. For socialism to triumph, the working class has to become more than just a _____, a category of people sharing the same economic position. In addition, it needs an awareness of its common position and a willingness to mobilize for change if it is to become a genuine _____.

44   Introduction to Sociology Study Guide

10. Marx suggested that two stages follow the revolution of the proletariat: first, a _____ phase, a dictatorship of the proletariat with the leaders of the revolution heading the political apparatus or the state. In the second stage, _____ is achieved and the state as a political force withers away.

11. While Marx stressed conflict, group (class) action, and the singular importance of economic power in understanding social stratification, the structural-functionalist school of thought emphasizes instead _____, _____, and _____ of power in modern social structures.

12. The author of the chapter, in agreement with Marx, argues that control of property and wealth, particularly by large businesses, is the most important source of _____ in modern stratification systems. In addition, following Weber, he suggests that the other two socioeconomic status hierarchies, _____ and _____, also play a key role in shaping the system of inequality.

13. The distribution of _____ is the most direct measure or indication of how groups or individuals rank in the overall stratification system.

14. The biggest occupational change this century has been the growth of _____ occupations and the corresponding decline of people working in _____.

15. In 1995, university graduates made about _____ as much in total income as did high school graduates.

16. The major subsystems, or _____ of society include the economy, polity, religion, education, and agents of social control.

17. Education is included among the set of socioeconomic status hierarchies, or power rankings, because it is closely linked to the acquisition of _____ and _____ in modern societies.

18. Generally the term _____ refers to the ability to lead a healthy, happy, and prosperous existence.

19. Overall, the _____ ethnic group still tends to dominate the top of the economic power structure in Canada. Two groups which historically have ranked consistently low in the stratification system are the _____ and _____.

20. Some have suggested that the extent and pervasiveness of female subordination in the stratification system is so great that the position of women is not unlike that of a _____.

Answers

KEY TERMS AND DEFINITIONS

1. class
2. proletariat
3. status set
4. class, status, party
5. intergenerational mobility
6. vertical mobility
7. achieved status
8. class in itself
9. social differentiation
10. status hierarchy
11. horizontal mobility
12. status
13. stratum
14. bourgeoisie, petite bourgeoisie
15. institutionalized power
16. status inconsistency
17. ascribed status
18. intragenerational mobility
19. status consistency
20. class for itself
21. social class
22. social stratification
23. power

SELF-QUIZ

1. b
2. c
3. b
4. b
5. a
6. d
7. c
8. a
9. c
10. b
11. e
12. b
13. d
14. b
15. d
16. c
17. d
18. b

FILL IN THE BLANKS

1. Toronto
2. 50 percent
3. feudal lord and serf; master and slave
4. curvilinear
5. vertical
6. class
7. Ontario, Atlantic
8. means of production
9. class in itself, class for itself
10. socialist, communism
11. consensus, individual action, pluralism
12. power, education, occupation
13. wealth
14. white collar, agriculture
15. twice
16. institutions
17. wealth, occupational status
18. life chances
19. British, French, Native peoples
20. minority group

CHAPTER 7

Gender Relations

OBJECTIVES

1. To understand gender from a social, macro-perspective called the gendered order, and from an individual perspective called gendered identity.

2. To appreciate the major theoretical perspectives now being applied to the study of gender.

3. To extend to gender roles the discussion of the nature-nurture debate developed in the socialization chapter.

4. To be familiar with the processes involved in gender socialization, including the role of language.

5. To be aware of the relationship between gender and such variables as work, health, aging, deviance, and poverty.

KEY TERMS AND DEFINITIONS

1. _____: the system of masculine dominance, through which masculine traits are privileged and males are systematically accorded greater access to resources and women are systematically oppressed.

2. _____: the tendency to communicate sexist messages, such as male superiority or the assumption that certain roles must be occupied by either males or females, through the use of language.

3. _____: the process of acquiring a gendered identity.

4. _____: role differentiation in which males and females are segregated, according to their sex, in the spheres of both paid and unpaid labour according to the belief that certain tasks are more appropriate for one sex than for the other.

5. _____: the view that women's real strength lies in their reproductive capacities, and that women's roles as wives and mothers are their true calling and source of status.

6. _____: the set of traits including emotionality, passivity, and weakness, seen by functionalists as associated with female roles of unpaid wife, mother, and homemaker, particularly as limited to the private sphere.

Chapter 7: Gender Relations 47

7. _____: the dual segregation of women into the pink-collar occupations outside the home, and to unpaid labour inside the home.

8. _____: the view that equality between the sexes can be achieved only through the abolition of male supremacy. Some of its advocates argue for female separatism and the abdication of women's reproductive role as the route to liberation.

9. _____: a biological category, either male or female, referring to physiological differences, the most pronounced of which involve the reproductive organs and body size.

10. _____: the view that gender inequality has its roots in the combined oppressiveness of patriarchy and capitalism.

11. _____: the tendency in Canadian society for women at all stages of the adult life cycle to be poorer than men, and to be trapped in lives of poverty.

12. _____: a social category, involving a continuum of traits ranging from "masculine" to "feminine," referring to the social expectations placed upon individuals on the basis of their biological sex.

13. _____: the self as it develops in accordance with the individual's gender and the social definitions of that gender within the larger gendered order.

14. _____: the widely held belief that females and males in our society are exclusively heterosexual, leading to labels of deviance if it is discovered they are not.

15. _____: the widespread belief and understanding that males are superior to females: that they are therefore more entitled to make decisions, to control resources, and generally to be in positions of authority.

16. _____: the set of norms specifying appropriate behaviour for males and females; those who violate them are generally labelled deviant.

17. _____: the sphere of unpaid domestic labour and biological reproduction, seen from a functionalist perspective as the preserve of females.

18. _____: the set of structural relations through which individual members of society are accorded different treatment on the basis of gender.

19. _____: the set of traits, including rationality, aggression, and strength, seen by functionalists as associated with the male roles of breadwinner and disciplinarian, particularly as limited to the public sphere.

20._____: the view that most structural inequality between women and men can be eradicated through the making of laws and the creation of social policies that will alter power relationships.

21._____: the sphere of paid labour and commerce, seen from a functionalist perspective as the preserve of males.

22._____: the way of thinking that sees females as close to the former and males to the latter.

23._____: to take a cultural product and treat it as if it were "natural."

SELF-QUIZ

1. The terms masculine and feminine are most closely associated with the concept of
   a) sex
   b) gendered order rather than gendered identity
   c) gender
   d) ascribed status
   e) transsexuality

2. The position most likely to define a gendered division of labour as acceptable is
   a) symbolic interactionism
   b) feminism
   c) socialist feminism
   d) radical feminism
   e) functionalism

3. Instrumentality does not include
   a) rationality
   b) aggression
   c) strength and domination
   d) emotionality
   e) breadwinning

4. Concerning sex-change operations, which of the following is false?
   a) there are more male to female than female to male operations
   b) electrolysis and estrogen may be used
   c) among men undergoing the operation, the greatest proportion are homosexuals and transvestites
   d) some men seek the operation to avoid the stigma of homosexuality
   e) an artificial penis may be constructed

5. Marx tended to a take a position similar to _____ on the question of the gendered division of labour.
   a) functionalists
   b) symbolic interactionists
   c) radical feminists
   d) liberal feminists
   e) the nurture side

6. A focus on day care and pay equity would be most characteristic of _____ feminism.
   a) maternal
   b) liberal
   c) socialist
   d) radical
   e) a to d are all the same on these issues

7. Individuals may be classified as masculine or feminine plus two other conditions, _____ and _____.
   a) bisexual and homosexual
   b) tomboy and sissy
   c) XX and XY
   d) androgynous and undifferentiated
   e) lesbian and gay

8. Which term is out of place with the others?
   a) heterosexual assumption
   b) gendered division of labour
   c) pink ghetto
   d) gender inclusive language
   e) feminization of poverty

9. Homeless women are drawn heavily from among
   a) former mental patients
   b) teenage runaways
   c) wives of homeless men
   d) a and b
   e) b and c

10. Women are in the majority for all of the following employee categories except
    a) sales
    b) clerical
    c) nurses
    d) service
    e) teaching

11. Even in 1996, women made just over _____ of what men did.

   a) 10%
   b) 30%
   c) 50%
   d) 70%
   e) 90%

12. In health matters, women do better than men in all of the following, except:

   a) declining smoking rates
   b) amount of stress experienced
   c) ability to handle stress
   d) exposure to poor work conditions
   e) longevity

13. Of the following, the most general term is

   a) gender norms
   b) ideology of gender inequality
   c) gendered order
   d) gender inclusive language
   e) double ghetto

14. Penis, vagina, and testes indicate that we are talking about

   a) gender
   b) sex
   c) masculine and feminine
   d) gender identity
   e) homosexuality

15. Identification as a transsexual would probably be best explained using

   a) maternal feminism
   b) conflict theory
   c) functionalism
   d) symbolic interactionism
   e) a and b

FILL IN THE BLANKS

1. The _____ is socially reproduced through the process of gender socialization.

2. It can be argued that sex is an _____ characteristic while gender is an _____ characteristic.

3. A major criticism of the functionalist view is that it justifies _____.

4. Going to work is an _____ task while nurturing is an _____ task.

5. A patriarch plus a homemaker and children would describe the Parsonian _____ family.

6. Transsexuals have a discrepancy between their gender identity and their biological sex. This is much more than _____, or wearing clothes of the other sex.

7. Unlike functionalism, symbolic interactionism focuses on the _____ of the different roles allocated to males and females.

8. _____ feminism is associated with a search for alternative reproductive strategies.

9. Women's work can be divided into three categories, _____, _____, and _____.

10. The term for Devor's masculine-appearing women is _____.

11. Some researchers have claimed that women are _____ brain dominant, men _____.

12. Bulimia and anorexia nervosa are manifestations of the _____, in which women's self-worth is particularly defined through their appearance.

13. On the good side, the "discovery" of _____ has led to the setting up of clinics to reduce its effects. On the bad side, it can be used to legitimate unequal treatment of men and women.

14. Approximately _____ percent of one-parent households are headed by females.

15. Of the four types of feminism listed, a religious conservative would most likely adopt _____.

Answers

KEY TERMS AND DEFINITIONS

1. patriarchy
2. linguistic sexism
3. gender socialization
4. gendered division of labour
5. maternal feminism
6. expressive dimension
7. double ghetto
8. radical feminism
9. sex
10. socialist feminism
11. feminization of poverty
12. gender
13. gendered identity
14. heterosexual assumption
15. ideology of gender inequality
16. gender norms
17. private realm
18. gendered order
19. instrumental dimension
20. liberal feminism
21. public realm
22. nature/culture dualism
23. naturalization of history

SELF-QUIZ

1. c
2. e
3. d
4. c
5. a
6. b
7. d
8. d
9. d
10. a
11. d
12. a
13. c
14. b
15. d

FILL IN THE BLANKS

1. gendered order
2. ascribed, achieved
3. an ideology of gender inequality
4. instrumental, expressive
5. head-complement
6. transvestism
7. social construction
8. Radical
9. wifework, motherwork, housework
10. gender blenders
11. left, right
12. cult of thinness
13. PMS
14. 80 (82)
15. maternal feminism

CHAPTER 8

Race and Ethnic Relations

OBJECTIVES

1. To understand the processes involved in the formation of an immigrant community.

2. To understand what is meant by ethnic, racial, and minority groups, especially in relation to the changing Canadian ethnic mosaic, and to become acquainted with such issues as prejudice, discrimination, and racism.

3. To become more fully aware of the history and pattern of First Nations/European colonizer and French/English relationships.

4. To understand three interpretations of ethnic group relations — assimilationism, two-category perspectives, and pluralism — and to consider some of the implications of each for social policy.

KEY TERMS AND DEFINITIONS

1. _____ : the view that ethnic diversity gradually and inevitably declines as group members are absorbed into the general population, in the process becoming more and more like the dominant group.

2. _____ : the development of a full set of institutions in an ethnic community that parallel those in the larger society.

3. _____ : an arbitrary social category based upon inherited physical characteristics, such as skin colour or facial features, and defined as socially meaningful.

4. _____ : mental images that exaggerate traits believed to be typical of members of a social group.

5. _____ : discrimination against members of a group that occurs as a by-product of the ordinary functioning of bureaucratic institutions, rather than as a consequence of a deliberate policy to discriminate.

6. _____ : a system of coexisting racial and ethnic groups, each of which maintains to some degree its own distinctive culture, networks, and institutions, while participating with other racial and ethnic groups in common cultural, economic, and political institutions.

7. _____ : the hierarchical ranking of ethnic populations in a society.

8. _____ : the learning of the language, values, and customs of a dominant group by an ethnic group.

9. _____ : the denial of opportunities, generally available to all members of society, to some because of their membership in a social category.

10. _____ : maintenance of physical distance between ethnic or racial groups.

11. _____ : a collection of individuals who share a particular trait that is defined as socially meaningful, but who may neither interact nor have anything else in common.

12. _____ : the domination by a settler society of a native or indigenous population. In time, the native population suffers the erosion of its traditional culture and usually occupies a subordinate status in the pluralist society of which it has involuntarily become a part.

13. _____ : a people — a collectivity of persons who share an ascribed status based upon culture, religion, national origin, or a shared historical experience based upon a common ethnicity or race.

14. _____ : prejudging people based upon characteristics they are assumed to share as members of a social category.

15. _____ : view of race relations that sees two, hierarchically ranked, separate collectivities in conflict, bound together in a relationship of dominance and subordination within a single society and culture.

16. _____ : sequential movement of persons from a common place of origin to a common destination, with the assistance of relatives or acquaintances already settled in the new location.

17. _____ : view that ethnic diversity, stratification, and conflict remain central features of modern societies, and that race and ethnicity continue to be important aspects of individual identity and group behaviour.

18. _____ : the collective designation given by assimilationists to four stages in the relationship between dominant and minority groups; stages are contact, competition, accommodation, and finally, assimilation.

19. _____ : a social category, usually ethnically or racially labelled, that occupies a subordinate rank in the social hierarchy.

20. _____ : the state of having within the self two conflicting social identities; also, the social condition of a minority group that lives on the edge of a society, not treated as a full member of that society.

21. _____ : acceptance of minority group by a dominant group into its intimate, primary, social relationships.

22. _____ : an ideology that regards racial or ethnic categories as natural genetic groupings and that attributes behavioural and psychological differences to the genetic nature of these groupings.

SELF-QUIZ

1. Immigrants who receive legal guarantees of support from relatives or others in Canada are classified as

    a) independent immigrants
    b) chain migration immigrants
    c) sponsored immigrants
    d) marginal immigrants
    e) *de jure* immigrants

2. One large factor in the development of a strong sense of solidarity, ethnic identity, and a wide range of institutions is

    a) cultural universals combined with minority group status
    b) the size of the ethnic population
    c) whether the individuals share similar values and beliefs
    d) the difference between achieved and ascribed status
    e) the experience of three solitudes

3. Weber and Barth both suggested that ethnicity has four major dimensions. Which of the following fits into their theoretical perspective?

    a) an achieved status
    b) a subculture
    c) an ascribed status
    d) a and b
    e) b and c

4. An important feature of an ethnic group as a form of social organization is that it

    a) has acculturated
    b) is fully isolated from the mainstream of society
    c) has boundaries
    d) lacks institutional completeness
    e) has assimilated into the mainstream of society

5. A 1990 survey by Decima found that _____ percent of Canadians agreed that "all races are created equal."

    a) 90
    b) 70
    c) 50
    d) 30
    e) 10

6. The term ethnogenesis refers to

    a) intense, informal interaction and communication among persons of the same ethnicity
    b) marriage within one's own ethnic group
    c) an ethnic group occupying an elite or privileged status
    d) the forcing of a common label and identity upon a group
    e) the passing on of genetic characteristics to one's ethnic group

7. The unemployment rate for First Nations people living off reserve is roughly _____ the rate for the rest of Canada.
   a) equal to
   b) double
   c) triple
   d) ten times
   e) one-half

8. Affirmative action targets include all of the following, except:
   a) women
   b) the disabled
   c) blacks in Nova Scotia
   d) French Canadians
   e) First Nations

9. Dominant groups frequently control and restrict the economic, social, and political participation of minorities by means of
   a) expulsion
   b) annihilation
   c) discrimination
   d) exploitation
   e) disruption

10. Which of the following statements is true?
    a) *de jure* discrimination is more frequent than *de facto* discrimination
    b) discriminatory behaviour is caused by prejudiced attitudes
    c) victims of prejudice usually bring it on themselves
    d) a prejudiced person may not discriminate and a person may discriminate yet not be prejudiced
    e) a and b only

11. Under the terms of the Indian Act, special status is conferred upon
    a) the Métis
    b) British Columbia and Manitoba Indians
    c) the Inuit
    d) registered Indians
    e) a and c only

12. The erosion of French language and culture in Canada has many complex sources. A main one is
    a) the recent increase in Quebec's death rate
    b) the fact that English-speaking immigrants to Canada far outnumber French-speaking immigrants
    c) the 1977 language legislation which specified that the language of Quebec's French majority shall be the official language of Quebec
    d) the victory of the federal Progressive Conservatives in the 1980s
    e) the economic recession of the 1990s

13. Post World War II immigration in Canada is marked by its
    a) ethnic networks
    b) institutional completeness
    c) ethnic diversity
    d) tendency toward cultural assimilation
    e) segregation of ethnic groups

14. Who is most likely to suffer marginality?
    a) a majority member who is increasingly outnumbered by minorities
    b) people who assimilate
    c) an immigrant
    d) colonists
    e) a and d

15. Endogamy is probably most important for which group below?
    a) Jews
    b) Italians
    c) Germans
    d) Ukrainians
    e) it is equally important to all groups listed

FILL IN THE BLANKS

1. _____ more than any other racial or ethnic group are likely to experience discrimination, according to a Toronto study.

2. *Nunavut* means _____ in Inuktitut.

3. Many observers predict not a bilingual Canada but a Canada of _____ solitudes.

4. In the media, minorities are defined as _____, in terms of race-role stereotyping, as a social problem, and as _____.

5. Pluralist societies in which peoples of various cultural, religious, or racial backgrounds live side by side within a single, social, economic, and political system exist as a consequence of the historical processes of _____, conquest, and _____.

6. A social attribute such as ethnicity, which is acquired from one's parents and other ancestors, and that is conferred at birth, is referred to as an _____.

7. Almost one in five Canadians, including many Italians and Chinese, have a _____ other than the two official languages.

8. The critical factor in the maintenance of ethnic group boundaries is _____, that is, marriage within one's own ethnic group.

9. The Charter of the French Language is better known as _____.

10. After the British and the French, the next largest group in Canada are the _____.

11. The two racial/ethnic groups in Toronto whose males experienced significantly lower incomes than the majority are the _____ and _____.

12. The _____ are those people descended from marriages between Indian women and early European settlers.

13. _____ is a system that is democratic for the master race but tyrannical for subordinate groups.

14. By setting a universalistic rule that all guards must weigh at least 150 pounds, a security firm may effectively be practising _____.

15. In intergroup relations, exaggerated mental images of groups are called _____, while the attitudes associated with these images are called _____, and the behaviour sometimes associated with them is called _____.

16. The _____ (1763) transferred virtually all Canadian lands under French control to the British.

17. The pattern of French settlement which entailed the granting of lands by the French crown to landowners who declared themselves vassals to the crown is known as the _____.

18. Columbus' calling the Native peoples of Canada "Indians" is an example of _____.

19. The era of the _____ immigrant was a brief one in Canada, for the predominant pattern of immigrant settlement has always been urban.

20. The perspective that maintaining one's immigrant ethnic culture and language will hinder upward mobility is called _____.

Answers

KEY TERMS AND DEFINITIONS

1. assimilationism
2. institutional completeness
3. race
4. stereotypes
5. systemic or institutionalized discrimination
6. pluralistic society
7. vertical mosaic
8. acculturation
9. discrimination
10. segregation
11. social category
12. colonialism
13. ethnic group
14. prejudice
15. two-category perspectives
16. chain migration
17. pluralism
18. race relations cycle
19. minority group
20. marginality
21. structural assimilation
22. racism

SELF-QUIZ

1. c
2. b
3. e
4. c
5. a
6. d
7. c
8. d
9. c
10. d
11. d
12. b
13. c
14. c
15. a

FILL IN THE BLANKS

1. Blacks
2. our land
3. two unilingual
4. invisible, amusement
5. colonialism, migration
6. ascribed status
7. mother tongue
8. endogamy
9. Bill 101
10. Germans
11. Chinese and West Indians
12. Métis
13. Herrenvolk democracy
14. institutionalized discrimination
15. stereotypes, prejudice, discrimination
16. Treaty of Paris
17. seigneurial system
18. ethnogenesis
19. farmer
20. assimilationism

CHAPTER 9

Aging

OBJECTIVES

1. To present a balanced portrayal of old age and aging, including its ups and downs.

2. To learn the various theoretical approaches to aging, including activity theory, disengagement theory, exchange theory, and others.

3. To understand the importance and sources of family ties and social support in later life, including siblings.

4. To be aware of the health and retirement issues facing older Canadians.

5. To know about the policy implications of the above.

KEY TERMS AND DEFINITIONS

1. _____: changes that are a direct function of aging; also called maturation.

2. _____: an interdisciplinary study of aging that involves the physical, psychological, and social processes related to growing old and being an older person.

3. _____: outcomes that result from having been a certain age at a certain point in time and that capture the impact of an historical time.

4. _____: a framework with several linking concepts, compatible with a number of theoretical approaches involving a series of age-related transitions that occur along a trajectory across the age structure.

5. _____: the study of the physiological aspects of aging and the unique health concerns of older persons.

6. _____: macro-level view of how certain processes create a structure that tends to place restraints on the lives of older people.

7. _____: view that the withdrawal of older persons from active social life (particularly from paid work) is functional for both the individual and for society.

8. _____: approach that emphasizes the subjective experience of older people and their ability to exercise agency in negotiations with others.

9. _____: a system of expectations and rewards based on age.

10. _____: examines power, social action, and social meanings as part of a critique of knowledge, culture, and the economy. It includes the social construction of old age, dependency, and old age policy.

11. _____: the view that the best prescription for a successful old age is to take on things that can supplant those left behind.

12. _____: a macro-level approach focused primarily on two key concepts: a structure that favours young and middle-aged adults and an age cohort, individuals who share the same age group.

SELF-QUIZ

1. By 2041, the percentage of Canadians over the age of 65 will be
    a) 3%
    b) 10%
    c) 23%
    d) 33%
    e) 50%

2. The term *praxis* is most closely associated with _____ theory.
    a) critical
    b) life course
    c) age graded
    d) disengagement
    e) activity

3. For women over the age of 75, the most common experience is
    a) divorce
    b) remarriage
    c) improved health
    d) moving in with a sibling
    e) widowhood

4. The _____ approach focuses on the ties between generations.
    a) social problems
    b) critical
    c) activity
    d) ambivalent
    e) solidarity perspective

5. Institutionalization in old age is more common among women, the never married, and the

   a) poor
   b) childless
   c) wealthy who can afford it
   d) divorced
   e) later born

6. About ___ percent of persons aged 65 and over have at least one living sibling.

   a) 10
   b) 33
   c) 50
   d) 80
   e) 99

7. Flexible age of retirement is associated with proponents of _____ justice and is mandatory with _____ justice.

   a) individual, comparative
   b) comparative, individual
   c) civil, tort
   d) feminist, patriarchal
   e) common law, civil

8. The average age of retirement in Canada is not 65 but

   a) 70
   b) 68
   c) 62
   d) 59
   e) 55

9. One-half of Canadians aged 65 years can expect to live another ___ years.

   a) 25
   b) 2
   c) 5
   d) 35
   e) 18

10. And ___ of these years should be disability free.

    a) one-half
    b) one-third
    c) most
    d) a few
    e) 4.5

FILL IN THE BLANKS

1. _____ analysis is concerned with the individal's experience of aging.

2. Everyone born in the compter age would experience similar _____ effects, not similar age effects.

3. Activity theory directly challenges _____ theory.

4. Individuals in the same age group constitute an _____.

5. The failure of society to adjust quickly to the growing numbers of years post-retirement is an example of a _____.

6. Some suggest that marriages follow a _____ pattern, with happiness greatest in the early and later years.

7. Research on physical activity reveals that one-half of the physical decline associated with age is due not to aging per se but to _____.

8. While young people arriving at hospital generally need short-term treatment for an acute problem, older people require a focus on _____ rather than cure.

9. Comparing 1971 and 1991, the trend is for _____ people working between the ages of 65 and 69.

10. Peronsal responsibility for aging issues would flow from Mills' concept of _____ rather than public issues.

11. Women retirees compared to men face more inadequate _____, while the men are challenged by a lack of social contacts.

12. The _____ is a supplement for pensioners with limited incomes. Some studies use qualifying for it as a measure of poverty.

Answers

KEY TERMS AND DEFINITIONS

1. age effects
2. gerontology
3. period effects
4. life course perspective
5. geriatrics
6. political economy of aging perspective
7. disengagement theory
8. social constructivist perspective
9. age-graded
10. critical theory
11. activity theory
12. age-stratification perspective

SELF-QUIZ

1. c
2. a
3. e
4. e
5. b
6. d
7. a
8. c
9. e
10. a

FILL IN THE BLANKS

1. Micro-level
2. period
3. disengagement
4. age cohort
5. structural lag
6. curvilinear
7. disuse
8. care
9. more
10. private troubles
11. financial security
12. GIS, Guaranteed Income Supplement

CHAPTER 10

Families

OBJECTIVES

1. To learn terms such as nuclear family, consanguine family, exogamy, polygamy, matriarchal, and patrilocal, to name a few, which reflect the variety of kinship and family forms.

2. To be aware of the differences in family patterns across societies.

3. To know both the macro- and micro-changes in functions performed by the family.

4. To understand the life cycle of the family, from socialization for marriage, to child-bearing, and child-rearing.

5. To appreciate the continuity in family forms, despite the great amount of change, including the greater prevalence of divorce.

KEY TERMS AND DEFINITIONS

1. _____: a woman's lesser power in a marriage partly arising from her generally being younger than her husband.

2. _____: the emotional dimension of marriage, including sexual gratification, companionship, and empathy.

3. _____: marriage of persons with similar physical, psychological, or social characteristics. This is the tendency for like to marry like.

4. _____: a commitment and an ongoing exchange. The commitment can include legal and social pressures against dissolution. The arrangement includes both instrumental and expressive exchanges.

5. _____: a nuclear family consisting of partners who are not legally married, with or without children.

6. _____: the task-oriented dimension of marriage, including earning a living, spending money, and maintaining a household.

7. _____: There are a variety of marital structures. In _____ marriages, a husband owns his wife; in _____ marriages, the wife finds meaning in life through her husband; in _____ marriages the wife is employed, but her job and income are less important than her husband's; and in _____ marriages, both spouses are equally committed to marriage and a career.

8. _____: There are also a variety of premarital sexual standards. The _____ standard allows no premarital sex; the _____ standard allows it for men only; the _____ standard permits premarital sex for persons if there is a strong personal commitment; and the _____ standard approves of it for both men and women, even without love.

9. _____: descent traced unilaterally through the male line; a child is related only to the father's relatives.

10. _____: one woman married to two or more men; wife-sharing.

11. _____: a family consisting of one parent and one or more children.

12. _____: the norm that marriage partners must be chosen from outside a defined group.

13. _____: marriage involving two or more men and two or more women.

14. _____: the residence pattern of couples who reside alone.

15. _____: a marriage relationship in which there is equal power of wife and husband.

16. _____: a family that includes more than spouses and unmarried children (e.g., grandparents, married children, other relatives) living in the same residence.

17. _____: norm that marriage partners must be members of the same group.

18. _____: couple takes up residence with the wife's parents.

19. _____: marriage involving more than two partners.

20. _____: people related by blood or marriage.

21. _____: males are the formal head and ruling power in the families.

22. _____: descent that follows both the male and female lines; a child is related to relatives of both parents.

23. _____: a family organization in which the primary emphasis is on biological relatedness (e.g., parents and children or brothers and sisters), rather than on the spousal relationship.

24. _____: marriage involving only two partners.

25. _____: society in which females are the formal head and ruling power in the families.

26. _____: two or more people related by blood, marriage, or adoption and residing together.

27. _____: one man married to two or more women; husband-sharing.

28. _____: descent traced unilaterally through the female line; a child is related only to the mother's relatives.

29. _____: couple takes up residence with the husband's parents.

30. _____: a family that includes only spouses and any unmarried children.

31. _____: marriage between two people who are dissimilar in some important regard, such as religion, ethnic background, social class, personality, or age.

32. _____: a nuclear family that includes children from more than one marriage or union.

33. _____: a nuclear family with children from a prior union of one of the spouses.

SELF-QUIZ

1. Cohabitation is generally

    a) patriarchal
    b) matriarchal
    c) polygynous
    d) neolocal
    e) hedonistic

2. For a unit to be called a family, the people involved must

    a) customarily live in the same dwelling
    b) be related
    c) be related and customarily live in the same dwelling
    d) be related by marriage or common-law union
    e) include at least one person of each sex

3. From anthropological data gathered in various societies, it is clear that only two types of marriage have been found with any frequency. They are

    a) group marriage and polygyny
    b) polygamy and monogamy
    c) monogamy and group marriage
    d) polygyny and polyandry
    e) monogamy and polygyny

4. In tribal societies
   a) the nuclear family is generally paramount
   b) reproduction is at a premium
   c) the consanguine family is generally paramount
   d) children are often spoiled
   e) b and c

5. Which of the following practices is the most uniform across societies?
   a) acceptance of extra-marital intercourse
   b) the incest taboo
   c) discouragement of premarital intercourse
   d) low premium on marriage
   e) endogamy

6. Which perspective looks at the family as one of the institutions of society and concentrates on instrumental exchanges?
   a) symbolic interactionism
   b) feminism
   c) structural functionalism
   d) social psychology
   e) conflict theory

7. What factor(s) most helped to decrease or change the functions previously performed by families?
   a) a reduced influence of religion and a decline in the birth rate
   b) industrialization
   c) the women's liberation movement and reactions to it
   d) the increase in the number of divorces
   e) a and d

8. The discussion about expressive exchanges concluded that
   a) the family has kept most of its economic, political, and religious functions
   b) the family has become more important as a source of emotional gratification for individuals
   c) families are more likely to stay together today than previously because they are a source of emotional gratification for individuals
   d) families are now quicker to break apart when individual members do not find a particular arrangement to be gratifying, a luxury they could not afford as providers of instrumental needs
   e) b and d

9. The probability of assault is about _____ times greater in common-law than in marital unions.
   a) four
   b) ten
   c) two
   d) the two probabilities are equal
   e) actually there is more assault in marital unions

10. Which standard of premarital sexuality received the greatest support among post-secondary students?

   a) love
   b) abstinence
   c) double
   d) fun
   e) all standards were equally supported

11. Most research on mate selection supports the following conclusion: mate selection or choice of marital partner tends to be

   a) homogamous
   b) heterogamous
   c) polygynous
   d) b and c
   e) a and c

12. Higher income _____ a woman's chances for divorce. It _____ a man's.

   a) decreases, increases
   b) has no effect on, decreases
   c) increases, decreases
   d) increases, has no effect on
   e) has no effect on, has no effect on

13. Researchers see cohabitation today as increasingly

   a) trial marriages
   b) a prelude to marriage
   c) a way to avoid divorce
   d) a substitute for marriage
   e) a way to reduce STDs

14. Which of the following is (are) false?

   a) because of the burdens of child-rearing, marriages involving children have a higher divorce rate than childless unions
   b) the younger the age at marriage, the greater the incidence of divorce
   c) because they have been hurt once already, people entering second marriages have a lower divorce rate than those entering first marriages
   d) women in senior-partner junior-partner marriages are more likely to divorce than those in head-complement marriages
   e) a and c

15. Which of the following statements is true?

   a) in the future, the institution of marriage may no longer exist
   b) the proportion of married people among the adult population is almost as high as ever
   c) childless couples will be the norm in the future
   d) in most marriages, men and women are equal partners
   e) a and c

FILL IN THE BLANKS

1. Marriages preceded by cohabitation have _____ rates of dissolution than those in which the couple do not live together before marriage.

2. Persons who customarily maintain a common residence but are not related form a _____ and not a family.

3. Murdock's research showed that polyandry is rare and when it occurs it is often _____ who share a wife.

4. The regulation of sexual behaviour outside of marriage shows variability across societies. Still, Murdock found that the majority of societies _____ premarital intercourse.

5. Most individuals are motivated to marry and they have the potential ability. What they lack is _____.

6. Concerning uniformity in family structure across societies, in most societies there is a high premium on _____. Another feature, almost uniform, is the incest taboo. Finally, the importance of _____ is found in most societies.

7. The decade sometimes called the "golden age of the family" is the _____.

8. What we are often seeing rather than an empty nest is that adult children still live at home, making it what some call a _____.

9. Today the functions of the family are largely limited to procreation, the raising of children, and to _____.

10. Nonindustrial societies were held together by _____, that is, by the sense of identity people had with their communities. In the industrial world, societies are held together by _____, a division of labour that allows individuals to profit from the specialized abilities of others.

11. Men who have lived by themselves apart from the nuclear family are more likely to marry. Are women who have lived alone more, less, or equally likely to marry than those who have not? _____

12. Beaujot noted that when both spouses work, childcare and housework are not equally shared. Women do about _____ percent, men about _____ percent.

13. In everyday conversations about mate selection, two contradictory principles often emerge: "opposites attract" and "like marries like." Which principle receives considerably more support? _____

14. Couples with young children at home are more likely to be _____ than are childless couples or those whose children have left home.

15. The potentially happy time period in a family that occurs after children have moved away is called the _____.

16. Relative power of spouses, although very difficult to measure, is another important aspect of marital interactions. It has been found that the power of the wife is _____ if she is at home with young children, and _____ when she is working.

___

Answers

KEY TERMS AND DEFINITIONS

1. mating gradient
2. expressive exchanges
3. homogamy
4. marriage
5. common-law union
6. instrumental exchanges
7. owner-property; head-complement; senior-partner junior-partner; equal partner
8. abstinence; double; love; fun
9. patrilineal
10. polyandry
11. single parent family
12. exogamy
13. group marriage
14. neolocal
15. equalitarian
16. extended family
17. endogamy
18. matrilocal
19. polygamy
20. kin
21. patriarchal
22. bilateral
23. consanguine family
24. monogamy
25. matriarchal
26. family
27. polygyny
28. matrilineal
29. patrilocal
30. nuclear family
31. heterogamy
32. blended family
33. reconstituted family

SELF-QUIZ

1. d
2. c
3. e
4. e
5. b
6. c
7. b
8. e
9. a
10. a
11. a
12. c
13. d
14. e
15. b

FILL IN THE BLANKS

1. higher
2. household
3. brothers
4. tolerate
5. knowledge of what is expected
6. marriage, inheritance
7. 1950s
8. cluttered nest
9. meeting the emotional needs of family members
10. mechanical solidarity, organic solidarity
11. less
12. 60, 40
13. like marries like
14. dissatisfied with their marriages
15. empty nest
16. lowest, highest

CHAPTER 11

Religion

OBJECTIVES

1. To appreciate the rapidly secularizing and changing religious life of Canadians, one that sets us apart from our nearest neighbour.

2. To understand Durkheim, Marx, and especially Weber's analysis of religion and social change with specific emphasis on the Protestant ethic and its relation to the growth of capitalism.

3. To be able to compare and contrast different forms of religious organizations, including: sect, church, denomination, ecclesia, and cult.

4. To be aware of Stark and Bainbridge's theory of religion and how it applies to Europe and North America.

5. To know the meaning of the term "invisible religion" and how it fits in with contemporary movements to make religion more individualistic, tolerant, and pragmatic.

KEY TERMS AND DEFINITIONS

1. _____: those things or experiences that appear to be inexplicable in terms of the laws of nature or the material universe.

2. _____: the attempt to reconcile and combine different philosophical and religious views, even some seemingly in conflict with each other.

3. _____: the sociological term for religious organizations that are well-established, inclusive (most can join), and involve involuntary membership, usually at birth.

4. _____: non-institutional and private expressions of religiosity in modern, largely secular societies.

5. _____: those objects and activities set apart by society and treated with awe and respect, often because of their association with gods or God.

6. _____: the process by which sectors of social life are removed from the domination of religious institutions and symbols.

7. _____: the sense people have of sharing in the overall intellectual heritage and wisdom of their culture while participating in religious rituals.

8. _____: the sense of excitement and power people experience when participating in lively events with a large crowd, such as religious revivals or rock concerts.

9. _____: the term for a very large, international religious organization that seeks to include everyone in the world in its membership.

10. _____: a type of religious organization characterized by a more exclusive orientation than churches, by voluntary membership, and by a more radical social outlook along with rigorous demands.

11. _____: in a religious context, the idea that people are born with certain abilities in order to fulfill, through their life's work, God's will.

12. _____: any definition that uses what religion does, not what it is, as its primary criterion.

13. _____: any definition that uses some conception of what religion essentially is, some key characteristic as its primary criterion.

14. _____: literally, all that is not sacred; in most cases, the world of everyday, non-religious experience.

15. _____: a church that dominates a society and considers itself to be the sole legitimate religion of that society.

16. _____: a system of beliefs and practices about transcendent things, their nature and consequences for humanity.

17. _____: practising self-discipline, especially doing without creature comforts, with a view to spiritual improvement.

18. _____: the belief that an all-knowing and all-powerful God determined from the dawn of creation who would be saved and who damned.

19. _____: in Weber's usage, a description of those things that are ordered, complex, and effective in their functioning; not magic or religious.

20. _____: a type of non-established religious organization based on voluntary membership. It is usually small and focused on the teaching of a charismatic leader.

21. _____: church-like religious organizations that recognize the legitimacy of other religious groups with which they compete for members.

SELF-QUIZ

1. Tyler's "belief in Spiritual Beings" is a _____ definition of religion.

    a) functional
    b) transcendent
    c) denominational
    d) substantive
    e) a, b, and c

2. The _____ refers to some level, type, or dimension of reality that is thought to be intrinsically different than and in some sense higher or beyond ordinary experience of the world.

    a) denominational
    b) ecclesiastic
    c) profane
    d) transcendent
    e) religious

3. In his discussion of the Arunta, Durkheim noted how all aspects of their lives were divided into two categories. The _____ possesses a tremendous power and provides a kind of fixed point in reality around which all else circulates.

    a) profane
    b) totems
    c) sacred
    d) rituals
    e) emblems

4. Which is not one of the eight dimensions of religious life according to Glock and Stark?

    a) ritualistic
    b) devotional
    c) ascetic
    d) communal
    e) belief

5. According to Weber, the spirit of capitalism was nourished by a combination of

    a) the accumulation of wealth and seeking of pleasure
    b) self-denial and the accumulation of wealth
    c) religious dogma and rational thinking
    d) the routinization of charisma and industrialization
    e) a and d

6. For Weber a society is more _____ if it displays a more specific and systematic approach to the acquisition and spread of ideas and information. It is more orderly, controlled, and efficient.

   a) ascetic
   b) capitalistic
   c) religious
   d) charismatic
   e) rational

7. Today's Jehovah's Witnesses are probably closest to which type of religious organization?

   a) church
   b) cult
   c) sect
   d) denomination
   e) ecclesia

8. Which of the following is true?

   a) denominations very often become ecclesia
   b) cults have been known to become sects
   c) ecclesia often turn into cults
   d) sects often become churches
   e) b and d

9. Organizations into which people are born and baptized as infants and whose membership is heterogeneous are called

   a) cults
   b) churches
   c) sects
   d) Pentecostals
   e) mystical

10. When religions become stagnant, when their rituals and beliefs become dead and hollow formalities disconnected from personal experience, there are two possible socio-religious responses, according to Stark and Bainbridge:

    a) mysticism and asceticism
    b) charisma and its routinization
    c) revival and innovation
    d) rationalization and compensation
    e) increased prayer and fasting

11. The rise of secular nationalism in Quebec and the decline of the power of the Roman Catholic Church came about largely as a result of

    a) urbanization
    b) mysticism
    c) asceticism
    d) increased church attendance
    e) The Quiet Revolution

12. _____ tend to be splinter groups from mainstream traditions that seek to revive what they think to be the original or pure spirit of the religious tradition they are rebelling against.

    a) Sects
    b) Cults
    c) Invisible religions
    d) Civil religions
    e) both c and d

13. _____ Canadians than Americans may be religious, but they are _____ truly religious.

    a) More, less
    b) More, much more
    c) Fewer, more
    d) Fewer, much less
    e) There are no differences in the religious experience of the two countries.

14. Estimates of the numbers involved in new religious movements, such as meditation and trance channelling, range from

    a) 0.5–1%
    b) 1–10%
    c) 20–25%
    d) 50–60%
    e) 90–100%

15. In new religions, traditional dualisms like God and humanity, spiritual and material, mind and body are replaced by a(n)

    a) invisible religion
    b) pragmatism
    c) mysticism
    d) denominationalism
    e) holistic approach

FILL IN THE BLANKS

1. According to Bibby, many Canadians are content to relegate religious matters to the periphery of their daily lives, and turn to religion only when necessary, for example to mark _____.

2. Durkheim saw the origin of religious experience and the source of religious power not in God but in _____.

3. Students with a strong spiritual orientation are more satisfied with their lives, experience better _____, and are better able to handle _____.

4. _____ prophecies about the ultimate end of humanity often play an important role in cult suicides.

5. The demonization of outsiders, the invention of crises, and the expelling of dissidents are used by leaders of cults to maintain their _____ authority.

6. Except in Quebec, the _____ religion is doing better than others in not losing its weekly attendance at religious services.

7. The *Celestine Prophecy* can be seen as part of the _____, associated with such practices as yoga, macrobiotics, telepathy, and astral projection.

8. The _____ dimension (Glock and Stark) measures the degree to which people think their religion is the one and only path to salvation.

9. While the majority of Canadians believe in God, heaven, and life after death, only about one-half believe in _____.

10. Promises of reward at some later time or in some other place, or _____, comprise Stark and Bainbridge's fourth premise in their theory of religion.

11. Christian _____ is growing today, stripped of its anti-religious overtones and delivered from a Christian perspective. New Life Clinics are an example.

12. Dogmatism, ritualism, and a hired leader are characteristic of a _____.

13. The liberal agenda of several Protestant groups in western Canada, also influential in the formation of the CCF, was called _____.

14. Wiccans and Neo-Pagans are contemporary adherents of _____. Many reject the reality of supernatural beings.

15. The transfer of authority from religion to economic, educational, medical, and other spheres is called _____. It can illustrate the evolution of society into ever-more complex parts.

Answers

KEY TERMS AND DEFINITIONS

1. supernatural
2. syncretism
3. church
4. invisible religion
5. sacred
6. secularization
7. collective conscience
8. collective effervescence
9. universal church
10. sect
11. calling
12. functional definition of religion
13. substantive definition of religion
14. profane
15. ecclesia
16. religion
17. ascetic
18. doctrine of predestination
19. rational
20. cult
21. denomination

SELF-QUIZ

1. d
2. d
3. c
4. c
5. b
6. e
7. c
8. e
9. b
10. c
11. e
12. a
13. c
14. b
15. e

FILL IN THE BLANKS

1. events in the life cycle, like birth and marriage
2. society itself
3. health, stress
4. Apocalyptic
5. charismatic
6. Roman Catholic
7. New Age Movement
8. particularistic
9. hell
10. compensators
11. psychotherapy
12. church
13. Social Gospel
14. witchcraft
15. institutional differentiation

CHAPTER 12

Media

OBJECTIVES

1. To understand the information revolution, its benefits, and its costs.

2. To learn how audiences react to the media, including the cultural studies position on this topic.

3. To appreciate the issues of gender representation in the media and media violence.

4. To be aware of the issues associated with the globalization of cyberspace.

KEY TERMS AND DEFINITIONS

1. _____: large corporations that combine many different media holdings, or have interests both in media and other industrial sectors.

2. _____: school of research that focuses on how people make meanings in everyday life, sometimes in ways resistant to the dominant values promoted by the major media.

3. _____: the use of computer networks such as the Internet for business purposes, primarily by creating direct links between producers and customers.

4. _____: a research method that extracts statistically significant data from a range of past studies.

5. _____: the idea that watching media violence, rather than stimulating real-life violence, provides a substitute or safety valve for aggression.

6. _____: an approach to mass media research that examines how individuals use the media to satisfy emotional or intellectual needs.

7. _____: the notion that audiences play an important role in interpreting or decoding media messages, often contrasted with the hypodermic model.

8. _____: a term originally used to critically describe the crass, conservative, and conformist tendencies of commercially organized mass entertainment, now often used approvingly to refer to business-driven media.

9. _____: the imaginary dimension in which we conceive of computer-mediated communication occurring.

10. _____: tendency of international communication flows to create cultural mixes or crossovers between previously distinct national and ethnic groups.

11. _____: the idea that heavy viewing of television leads people to perceive reality in ways consistent with what they see on television.

12. _____: popular term for the integration of computers, telecommunications, and other digital technologies into a society-wide network.

13. _____: the imposition of one nation's way of life on another, not through direct occupation but by the indirect effects of media influence.

14. _____: a term applied to the alleged tendency for repeated exposure to media violence to make people increasingly indifferent to or accepting of such incidents in real life.

15. _____: the belief that media shoot powerful messages into weak, passive audiences, thus directly controlling their behaviour.

16. _____: the idea that new technologies drive social change.

17. _____: approach to communication studies focusing on the power relations governing the production, distribution, and consumption of information.

18. _____: a new stage of civilization supposedly being brought into being by computers and telecommunications, succeeding the old industrial society.

19. _____: a phrase suggesting that computers and other digital technologies empower citizens by allowing them to create and circulate information for themselves.

20. _____: the disparity between the capacities of the developed and less developed world to produce and distribute information.

21. _____: a group of computer users separated geographically but linked together in cyberspace by shared interests and concerns.

22. _____: the idea that viewing media violence encourages people to shed their restraints against committing real-life violence.

SELF-QUIZ

1. "The medium is the message" means that it is the _____ of communication and not its _____ that is important.

    a) amount, content
    b) content, amount
    c) form, amount
    d) content, form
    e) form, content

2. In McLuhan's view, _____ was linked to excessive rationality, linear thinking, and a split between the head and heart.

    a) the oral tradition
    b) radio
    c) cyberspace
    d) electronic media
    e) printing

3. Bell's _____ society, which would be propelled by advances in scientific knowledge, is roughly equivalent to the information society.

    a) pre-industrial
    b) post-industrial
    c) industrial
    d) global
    e) none of the above

4. The post-industrial society would be marked by all of the following, except:

    a) intellectual technology
    b) so much social change predictions would become harder
    c) a service economy
    d) technical rather than manual work
    e) b and c

5. Attractive to the political right and to the left is the _____ model that sees the audience either as passive zombies or as glassy-eyed dupes.

    a) effects
    b) uses and gratification
    c) hypodermic
    d) cultural studies
    e) cybernetics

6. Men's style of television viewing is characterized by all of the following, except:

    a) systematic
    b) silent
    c) uninterrupted
    d) unshared
    e) watching while doing something else

7. _____ exists where a corporation owns different stages or steps in a related economic process, such that companies under the same owner supply and consume each other's products.

   a) A cartel
   b) A virtual community
   c) A transnational
   d) Horizontal integration
   e) Vertical integration

8. Some question the "Gutenberg Revolution" because the _____ invented mechanical printing.

   a) Romans
   b) Greeks
   c) Chinese
   d) Americans
   e) Egyptians

9. Chomsky and Hermann argued that five filters allow the US media to control the thought of the populace. They do not include

   a) "flak"
   b) the Internet
   c) anti-communism as national secular religion
   d) a reliance on advertising as the primary income source
   e) the dependency of the media on information provided by outside experts

10. While closer with respect to _____ and especially _____, Europeans actually have significantly more _____ and _____ per capita than North Americans.

    a) books published, television sets, daily newspapers, radios
    b) daily newspapers, radios, books published, television sets
    c) books published, daily newspapers, radios, television sets
    d) radio, television sets, daily newspapers and books published
    e) television sets, camcorders, Internet access, CD players

FILL IN THE BLANKS

1. Television, according to McLuhan, with its immediacy and intimacy, retribalizes humankind but on a planetary scale, creating the _____ .

2. Some talk about the post-industrial society, some the network society, some the web society. But the most common term is the _____.

3. Political economists are concerned because, despite the multiplicity of media outlets, all transmit a common corporate-speak that depicts an air-brushed _____ while they hide issues of injustice.

4. The view that media audiences were inert and manipulated, with a linear connection between the messages and people's behaviour, is a central tenet of the _____.

5. Cultural studies includes the concept of a _____ reading of the news, one that accepts the broad picture but with some qualification relating to personal interest of the audience member.

6. _____ were structured to fit the rhythm of housework, scheduled to punctuate the day, but designed to allow distracted viewing.

7. Men tend to choose programs with _____ content on television while women choose those which are _____.

8. While "sex sells" it is just as important that _____, a fact that may lead to more equitable treatment of women and sexual minorities.

9. Vicarious experience of violence, such as that found in playing a gory video game, is a central argument in _____ theory.

10. The type of doll used in experimentally testing the effects of viewing violence is called _____.

11. The fact that Rupert Murdoch had to back away from imposing Western style programming in India to include a more local variety, including Hindi music, is evidence against the _____ argument sometimes levelled at the West.

12. The placeless, global consumer capitalism is also referred to as _____. It squeezes out any form of cultural production that is not for sale.

13. Some fear that in the new virtual world people will go from being couch potatoes to _____.

14. _____ is the term invented by Gibson, the Canadian science fiction author.

15. Users of the Internet tend to be drawn from different groups and not from others. _____, _____, and _____ are under-represented.

Answers

KEY TERMS AND DEFINITIONS

1. communication conglomerates
2. cultural studies
3. virtual commerce
4. meta-analysis
5. surrogate theory
6. uses and gratification model
7. active audience theory
8. culture industry
9. cyberspace
10. hybridization
11. cultivation effect
12. information highway
13. cultural imperialism
14. desensitization
15. hypodermic model
16. technological determinism
17. political economy of media
18. information society
19. technologies of freedom
20. information imbalance
21. virtual community
22. disinhibition

SELF-QUIZ

1. e
2. e
3. b
4. b
5. c
6. e
7. e
8. c
9. b
10. d

FILL IN THE BLANKS

1. global village
2. information society
3. happy consumerism
4. "effects" school
5. negotiated
6. Soaps
7. factual, fiction
8. "money talks"
9. surrogate
10. Bobo
11. cultural imperialism
12. McWorld
13. mouse potatoes
14. Cyberspace
15. Women, the poor, ethnic minorities

CHAPTER 13

Work and Organizations

OBJECTIVES

1. To grasp a new definition of the human activity of work, and examine its effect upon people. How is it different from non-human work?

2. To understand the relationship between formal organizations and their informal counterparts.

3. To understand the strengths and weaknesses of the modern detailed division of labour.

4. To appreciate the various forms of labour resistance, the role of unions in them, and the effects of globalization of work on them.

KEY TERMS AND DEFINITIONS

1. _____: the process by which a company reduces its labour force in order to reduce operating costs.

2. _____: working not for the enjoyment of the job but for the money that then translates into life enjoyment.

3. _____: Michels' idea that the leadership of even democratic organizations becomes elitist; rule by the many becomes rule by the few.

4. _____: a system that seeks to transfer control of the work process from the workers to the managers and owners. It is built upon a detailed division of labour that is perceived of as leading to "efficiency."

5. _____: breaking a task down into sub-tasks which are then given to different people who can be more easily trained and paid less than someone who might produce a full product.

6. _____: assembly line process of mass production to facilitate mass consumption, so named because of its developer.

7. _____: the socially sanctioned understanding that if people work hard and produce more goods and services each year, the economy will grow, benefitting all financially, both workers and owners.

8. _____: the division of jobs among people to ensure societal survival and prosperity.

9. _____: a special type of formal organization characterized by written rules and a hierarchical authority. It emphasizes impersonal work relationships, technical knowledge, and rationality.

10. _____: marked by a division of labour and set up to achieve a goal or goals, they include hospitals and political parties.

11. _____: as developed by Marx, it describes the separation of workers from the product of their labour, as well as from the process of work, fellow workers, and even the basic traits of humanity.

12. _____: the rules and groups that arise to meet the challenges of complex day-to-day life in formal organizations.

SELF-QUIZ

1. Worker resistance to change is more likely when the following occur, except:
    a) they do not understand what is going on
    b) their security is jeopardized
    c) changes have been forced upon them
    d) they have no stake in the new system
    e) the informal organization has become bureaucratized

2. The idea of a social construction of reality is most relevant to the _____ aspect of organization.
    a) bureaucratic
    b) formal
    c) informal
    d) complex division of labour
    e) industrial

3. One thing that distinguishes human work from that performed by animals is the human
    a) division of labour
    b) class consciousness
    c) greater rationality
    d) ability to conceptualize
    e) skill

4. _____ theorists point out that individuals create temporary agreements and informal understandings with co-workers to facilitate the completion of their jobs.
    a) Informal organization
    b) Formal organization
    c) Marxist
    d) Negotiated order
    e) Symbolic interactionist

5. Durkheim's term for the condition arising out of the division of labour that leaves people feeling atomized and experiencing normlessness is _____.

   a) charisma
   b) anomie
   c) mechanical solidarity
   d) organic solidarity
   e) alienation

6. Approximately what percentage of the contracts that come up for negotiation are settled without a strike?

   a) 25%
   b) 33%
   c) 50%
   d) 75%
   e) 95%

7. Which of the following is not a characteristic of Weber's concept of bureaucracy?

   a) expert training
   b) hierarchy
   c) flexible rules
   d) written documents
   e) official jurisdictional areas

8. The main reason(s) for the tendency toward oligarchy according to Michels is (are)

   a) the psychological needs of the leaders to maintain power
   b) the need of workers to be motivated more by social than economic rewards
   c) the need of the public to be guided
   d) a and b
   e) a and c

9. Which could be accused of manipulating workers?

   a) Taylorism
   b) Fordism
   c) Total Quality Management and Continuous Quality Improvement
   d) bureaucratic theory
   e) scientific management

10. The social contract in Canada is in trouble for several reasons. Of the following, which is not a reason?

    a) free trade agreements
    b) globalization of production
    c) reduction in government spending
    d) the increasingly detailed division of labour
    e) b and c only

11. Unemployment in Canada is increasing, but not because of

   a) greater power in the informal organization
   b) the decline of mass production
   c) the movement of jobs to Third World countries
   d) less government intervention into the economy
   e) the reduction in the civil service

12. In Canada in the 1990s, there has been close to ___ percent official unemployment.

   a) 10
   b) 20
   c) 2
   d) 5
   e) 30

13. The theoretical foundation of negotiated order theory is found in

   a) ethnomethodology
   b) functionalism
   c) symbolic interactionism
   d) conflict theory
   e) the writings of Durkheim

14. It is the _____ problem that is foremost on the agenda for the study of work in the new millennium.

   a) equity
   b) sustainable environment
   c) bureaucracies
   d) lack of work
   e) two wage earner family

15. Bureaucracy is not marked by

   a) a division of labour
   b) power structure chain of command
   c) informal aspects being paramount
   d) written communication
   e) tenure

FILL IN THE BLANKS

1. Rumour mills remind us that informal networks are not always positive but can be _____ as well.

2. A special type of formal organization, one particularly characteristic of the modern world and sometimes called "the iron cage," is a _____.

3. Compared to animals, human creation is based not on _____ but on _____.

4. Evolution and then the human capacity for _____ created a strong pressure for the more agile human intellect.

5. In hunting and gathering societies, families divided jobs by gender, called a _____ division of labour.

6. According to Marx, _____ is a structural problem, rooted in the relationship between the managers and the managed, the deciders and the doers.

7. Strikes, working to rule, and avoiding or slowing management directions are all part of what can be called _____.

8. _____ was Weber's concept for the movement away from magical or sacred interpretations of the world.

9. Taylorism, job insecurity, powerlessness, poor working conditions with long hours, but most of all a requirement that the employer collect the dues all led to an increase in _____ after World War II.

10. Involving workers in the decision-making process was more successful in Japan than here because their society is more _____. Here we have distrust.

11. Shortening the work week, early retirement, restricted overtime, and job sharing are designed to deal with our problem of _____.

12. The _____ thesis argues that the human ability to use tools in the process of work develops the human capacity for conceptualization that leads to more work with tools, etc.

13. Taylor argued that all _____ must be removed from the shop floor and placed in the hands of management.

14. The four-word, weekly occurring sentiment that typifies instrumentalism is _____.

15. The *Masters and Servants Act* and the *Anti-Combines Act* were used to thwart the development of _____.

Answers

KEY TERMS AND DEFINITIONS

1. downsizing
2. instrumentalism
3. iron law of oligarchy
4. scientific management
5. detailed division of labour
6. Fordism
7. social contract
8. social division of labour
9. bureaucracy
10. formal organizations
11. alienation
12. informal organization

SELF-QUIZ

1. e
2. c
3. d
4. d
5. b
6. e
7. c
8. e
9. c
10. d
11. a
12. a
13. c
14. d
15. c

FILL IN THE BLANKS

1. dysfunctional
2. bureaucracy
3. instinct, learning
4. language
5. social
6. alienation
7. resistance
8. Disenchantment of the world
9. union membership
10. collectivist
11. unemployment
12. Washburn
13. brainwork
14. thank God it's Friday
15. unions

CHAPTER 14

Social Movements

OBJECTIVES

1. To understand the meaning of the general term "collective behaviour" and its specific forms: panics, crowds, fads, crazes, publics, and social movements.

2. To understand the collective behaviour perspective on social movements, including Blumer's and Smelser's work, as well as emergent-norm theory and game theory.

3. To compare and contrast other theoretical perspectives on social movements — the social breakdown approach, the relative deprivation approach, the collective action approach, and postmodernism and the new social movement approach.

4. To be aware of the principal cleavages and integrative bonds that have shaped the character of collective action in Canada, with emphasis on regional and ethnic cleavages.

KEY TERMS AND DEFINITIONS

1. _____: activity in which a large number of people reject and/or do not conform to conventional ways of acting. Behaviour of this kind is often described as less "institutionalized" than ordinary behaviour.

2. _____: a large and dispersed group made up of persons who share an interest in the same thing. They may hold similar views, or they may sharply disagree.

3. _____: large collectivities of people trying to bring about or resist social change. Sociologists often assume that they are the most institutionalized form of collective behaviour.

4. _____: a special type of interaction in which responses are reinforced among people. The behaviour of one individual stimulates a response in another person, which in turn reinforces the tendency of the first person, and so on.

5. _____: over-simplified notions that, according to Smelser, give rise to collective behaviour. They portray the world in terms of omnipotent forces, conspiracies, or extravagant promises.

6. _____: the attachment of individuals to social groups or institutions. It depends on a set of sanctions that rewardsconformity to group norms and punish non-conformity.

7. _____: an explanation of crowd behaviour that stresses diversity of membership but also a perception of consensus that leads to a new norm expressing the apparent will of the crowd.

8. _____: an approach to collective behaviour that argues that social unrest occurs when established institutions are disrupted or weakened.

9. _____: the rapid and uncontrolled spread of a mood, impulse, or form of conduct through a collectivity of people.

10. _____: an explanation of crowd behaviour similar to emergent-norm theory, except that it assumes that people conduct themselves in a "rational" manner and on the basis of relative costs and payoffs.

11. _____: a movement in the 1960s in Quebec to expand governmental powers, to decrease church power, to modernize Quebec, and to fight vigorously for *la survivance*.

12. _____: the pursuit of goals by more than one person. As an explanation of social movements, it looks at integration and cleavage factors and seeks to explain variations in collective action.

13. _____: the transfer of resources, particularly human resources, from the pursuit of one goal or set of goals to the pursuit of another goal or set of goals.

14. _____: an unconventional practice that is adopted by a large number of individuals, but is regarded as strange by most people in the society. It is generally more outlandish than a fad and therefore requires greater personal commitment.

15. _____: a division (based on age, class, or ethnicity, etc.) that may result in the formation of distinct social groups.

16. _____: a temporary group of people in reasonably close physical proximity. Only unconventional ones are included under the heading of collective behaviour.

17. _____: a set of beliefs that helps people to interpret and explain their world and that provides the basis for collective action.

18. _____: an unconventional practice that spreads rapidly and is adopted in a short period of time by a large number of people. Generally less outlandish than a craze, it requires less personal commitment.

19. _____: the difference between what people believe they have a right to receive (their *expectations*) and what they actually receive (their *achievements*).

20._____: a rapid and impulsive course of action that occurs when people are frightened and try to save themselves or their property from perceived danger.

21._____: survival of French Canada as a distinct society.

22._____: the individual benefits that a person can derive from belonging to an association or joining a social movement. They help motivate people to join social movements.

23._____: the domination of a class or classes over others, not only economically but politically and culturally as well

24._____: a pattern of relationships among individuals or groups in a society that usually changes only slowly. For example, the kinship structure of a society refers to the most commonly found relations among relatives and married persons in a society. Social stratification is the structure of inequality in a society.

SELF-QUIZ

1. Organizations for specific purposes, such as pensioners' associations and feminist organizations, in the text were called

    a) publics
    b) social movements
    c) crazes
    d) status columns
    e) crowds

2. _____ is usually the major reason that people engage in protest activities.

    a) Cleavage
    b) Anger
    c) Relative deprivation
    d) Rising expectations
    e) Social integration

3. Blumer argued that the fundamental process(es) underlying crowd behaviour is (are)

    a) interpretive behaviour
    b) panic
    c) social contagion
    d) circular reaction
    e) c and d only

4. Which of the following does not describe new social movements?

   a) social breakdown
   b) anti-authority
   c) less economic than old movements
   d) concerned with values and culture
   e) spontaneous and decentralized

5. Which of the following is (are) a criticism of Smelser's work?

   a) there is insufficient evidence to show that circular reaction is characteristic of collective behaviour
   b) its suggestion that participants are swept up in a common mood is not demonstrated
   c) it implies that the motivations and aims of those who engage in collective behaviour are the illusions of irrational minds
   d) a and b only
   e) a and c only

6. Bourassa thought the special mission of French Canadians was to preserve above all their

   a) language
   b) culture
   c) religion
   d) institutions
   e) economy

7. Which of the following is a criticism of the collective behaviour tradition?

   a) too much attention is given to social structure
   b) too little attention is spent on interest groups and the conflicts among them
   c) too much attention is spent on mobilization factors
   d) it ignores the distinguishing feature of social movements, that is, their lack of institutionalization
   e) none of the above

8. According to the collective-action perspective, two kinds of factors are necessary for the occurrence of social movements. They are

   a) social breakdown and relative deprivation
   b) discontent and consensus
   c) cleavage factors and integrating factors
   d) mobilization factors and discontent
   e) social breakdown factors and socially isolated individuals

9. De Tocqueville thought that a major factor underlying the French Revolution was

   a) rising expectations
   b) discontent
   c) dissatisfaction
   d) circular reaction
   e) contagion

10. Social cleavage between regions, combined with social integration within regions, has resulted in collective action that tends to be weak and divided _____, while often strong _____.

   a) nationally, regionally
   b) regionally, nationally
   c) individually, socially
   d) politically, economically
   e) b and d

11. Nationally, the Progressive Movement did not survive long as an independent political force because

   a) it relied too heavily on religious broadcasts to attract followers
   b) its leader died and the routinization of charisma failed
   c) it was too local, drawing its strength primarily from the prairie provinces
   d) it was taken over by the CCF
   e) b and c

12. Which political party charged that eastern business elites were controlling and manipulating the economy to serve their interests?

   a) CCF
   b) NDP
   c) Social Credit
   d) Communist
   e) none of the above

13. Which group focuses on differences and discontinuities; denounces positivism and stresses indeterminacy; and rejects large, embracing theories that try to explain everything?

   a) postmodernists
   b) neo-Marxists
   c) collective action theorists
   d) relative deprivation theorists
   e) game theorists

14. The point of the boxed insert on food rioters is that crowd behaviour is

   a) wild and senseless
   b) logically patterned
   c) evolutionary
   d) more like a craze than a fad
   e) countercultural

15. Nationalism has long been popular among the Québecois. Before the Quiet Revolution, the survival of French Canada was to be achieved by

   a) advocating separation from the rest of Canada
   b) keeping people loyal to traditional values
   c) strengthening ties with France
   d) accepting the processes of urbanization and industrialization
   e) maintaining tight control over the provincial government

FILL IN THE BLANKS

1. In contrast to relative deprivation theory, collective action argues that discontent is perhaps a _____ condition but not a _____ condition for social unrest.

2. In resource mobilization theory, the function of a _____ is to identify a problem, diagnose it, attribute blame, and offer a solution.

3. According to social breakdown theory, _____, _____ and _____ individuals are most likely to participate in social unrest.

4. Collective action theorists argue that it is more important to study the _____ rather than the amount of social unrest.

5. The two categories of revolts in which Marxists are interested are those that led to the overthrow of _____, called bourgeois revolts, and those that Marx hoped would lead to the overthrow of _____.

6. The theory that can best explain why many different people would begin to believe in something like recycling or Echinacea is _____.

7. Framing, leadership, effective means of communication, cooperative relationships, and financial resources are each part of the larger process of _____, a key factor in the collective action approach.

8. There is a widespread supposition in sociological writings that social unrest occurs when established institutions are _____.

9. One of the significant contributions of Gramsci has been to persuade Marxists of the importance of _____ struggles against the existing order.

10. Until the 1990s, collective action by Indians and Inuit in Canada was characterized by considerable _____, which allowed other Canadians to rule them without serious opposition.

11. Collective _____ refers to relatively non-institutionalized conduct, i.e., conduct that departs from the ordinary and routine. In contrast, collective _____ covers both institutionalized and non-institutionalized activity.

12. The term _____ includes student, urban, feminist, environmental, gay, and lesbian varieties.

13. We learn about the views of a _____ by studying the results of political elections, calls to phone-in shows, letters to newspapers, etc.

14. The "Regina Manifesto" is associated with the _____.

15. Those patterns of differentiation that have had the most effect on collective action in Canada are: _____, _____, _____, _____, _____, and _____.

Answers

KEY TERMS AND DEFINITIONS

1. collective behaviour
2. public
3. social movements
4. circular reaction
5. generalized beliefs
6. social integration
7. emergent-norm theory
8. social breakdown approach
9. social contagion
10. game theory
11. Quiet Revolution
12. collective action
13. mobilization
14. craze
15. social cleavage
16. crowd
17. frame
18. fad
19. relative deprivation
20. panic
21. *la survivance*
22. selective incentives
23. hegemony
24. social structure

SELF-QUIZ

1. d
2. b
3. e
4. a
5. c
6. c
7. b
8. c
9. a
10. a
11. c
12. c
13. a
14. b
15. b

FILL IN THE BLANKS

1. necessary, sufficient
2. frame
3. alienated, uprooted, socially maladjusted
4. character
5. feudalism, capitalism
6. emergent-norm theory
7. mobilization
8. disrupted or weakened
9. non-economic, including ideological
10. factionalism
11. behaviour, action
12. new social movements
13. public
14. CCF
15. age, socioeconomic status or class, ethnicity, region, rural or urban residence, gender

CHAPTER 15

Demography and Urbanization

OBJECTIVES

1. To learn the basic variables of population study — fertility, mortality, and migration — and the part each plays, in conjunction with other social, cultural, and economic factors in social life.

2. To understand several theoretical perspectives on population change — demographic transition theory and the views of Malthus and Marx.

3. To be aware of different measures of mortality, fertility, and migration, and to know the factors related to these variables in a Canadian context, past and present.

4. To appreciate patterns of urbanization in the developed and developing world.

KEY TERMS AND DEFINITIONS

1. _____: measure for the average number of children a woman (or group of women) will have in their lifetime.

2. _____: indicators that measure demographic behaviour during a particular time period, such as a year or decade.

3. _____: a measure derived from a life table estimating the average length of life for persons exposed to a given set of age-specific death rates.

4. _____: Malthus' term for those occurrences like war, famine, and disease that reduce overpopulation.

5. _____: a measure based on the ratio of persons under 15 or over 65 to those in the working ages 15–64.

6. _____: a measure of childbearing rates computed by dividing the number of births to women of a particular age group by the total number of women in that age group.

7. _____: a fertility measure computed by dividing the total number of births in a time period by the total size of the population.

8. _____: movement across legally defined boundaries; can be internal or international.

9. _____: Malthus' checks to overpopulation that reduce the number of conceptions, such as abstinence and later marriage.

10. _____: the idea that populations pass through a three-stage process, from relatively high fertility and mortality levels, to high fertility but low mortality, to low fertility and mortality.

11. _____: a measure of population growth based on the difference between the crude birth rate and the crude death rate.

12. _____: measure of mortality that divides the number of deaths of people of a particular age by the total number of people of that age.

13. _____: the academic discipline that studies population processes.

14. _____: mortality measure computed by dividing the total number of deaths in a time period by the total population.

15. _____: a graphic illustration of the proportion of the population in each age-sex category.

16. _____: indicators that measure behaviour over time of a group of people who share a common starting point, such as year of birth or date of marriage.

17. _____: a statistical model based upon the probability of dying at given ages estimating the average number of years of life remaining for persons of varying ages.

SELF-QUIZ

1. To understand the magnitude of world population growth, remember that the world adds to its total population weekly the size of the city of _____.

    a) Regina
    b) Mexico City
    c) Toronto
    d) Vancouver
    e) Fredericton

2. Stage I of the demographic transition is characterized by

    a) high fertility, low mortality
    b) low fertility, low mortality
    c) high fertility, high mortality
    d) low fertility, high mortality
    e) none of the above

3. Today's developing nations are at a disadvantage in trying to duplicate the European experience of the demographic transition because

   a) the decrease in mortality occurred too quickly for them to adjust
   b) there is a dramatic increase in their fertility but not a corresponding increase in mortality
   c) new methods of birth control are required there
   d) they are stuck in stage I of the demographic transition
   e) they prefer positive to preventive checks

4. Malthus based his ideas on the relationship of population to the social and economic world. Which of the following could not be one of his arguments?

   a) population invariably increases when the means of subsistence increase
   b) new methods of birth control for males must be developed to keep population in check
   c) population is necessarily limited by the means of subsistence
   d) checks to population growth include vice, war, and famine
   e) a and c

5. While about half of Canadians change their residence at least once during a five-year period, _____ percent move to a different province.

   a) 60
   b) 50
   c) 33
   d) 25
   e) 5

6. Which of the following is a criticism of Malthus' theory of overpopulation?

   a) he overestimated the advances the Agricultural Revolutions would make in food production
   b) he defined the level of subsistence too specifically
   c) he would and could not foresee the widespread application of birth control
   d) he focused his attention too heavily on capitalist structure rather than on individual initiative
   e) b and d

7. While the rate of natural increase in European societies never surpassed 2 percent, in some developing countries today it has reached _____ percent, doubling every 17 years.

   a) 40
   b) 30
   c) 20
   d) 10
   e) 4

8. Reaching retirement age is the norm in Canada. In fact almost _____ percent of young Canadians can expect to celebrate their sixty-fifth birthday
   a) 90
   b) 80
   c) 70
   d) 60
   e) 50

9. Which country is the near perfect example of the kind of change predicted by demographic transition theory?
   a) Thailand
   b) China
   c) Mexico
   d) India
   e) South Korea

10. According to mortality differentials, which of the following individuals of equal age is probably likely to die first?
    a) a married male from a middle socioeconomic status
    b) a divorced female of French origin
    c) a single male from a low socioeconomic status
    d) a married female from a low socioeconomic status
    e) a divorced male from a middle socioeconomic status

11. Which of the following is probably overall the most important explanatory factor in variations of number of children born?
    a) ethnic background
    b) social class
    c) rural/urban location
    d) education
    e) religion

12. Which of the following was not a major cause of mortality decline in Western countries?
    a) better nutrition
    b) modern medicine
    c) better sanitation
    d) an improved standard of living
    e) a, c, and d

13. The world's crude birth rate today is about
    a) 38
    b) 28
    c) 24
    d) 14
    e) 4

14. In Western societies, which of the following has the greatest, perhaps unintended, effect on fertility?
   a) breastfeeding
   b) abstinence
   c) marriage patterns; later marriage reduces fertility
   d) migration
   e) urbanization

15. A population-pyramid
   a) provides information on the average number of years any individual can expect to live upon reaching a certain age
   b) reveals if a society has an old or a young population
   c) allows one to study society in terms of distribution, composition, and change
   d) gives information pertaining to the internal migration of people
   e) gives information pertaining to the number of neonatal and perinatal deaths per year in a population

FILL IN THE BLANKS

1. Demography's primary variables are _____, _____, and _____.

2. _____ refers to the biological potential to bear children, not to actual childbearing.

3. It is clear that population growth on a world scale is a function of the relationship between only two things: _____ and _____.

4. Stages two and three of the demographic transition can be summarized as follows:

   Stage II: _____ fertility + _____ mortality = _____ increase.

   Stage III: _____ fertility + _____ mortality = _____ increase.

5. While as late as 1960 births to unmarried mothers was about 4 percent of total, today the figure is closer to _____ percent, and in Quebec even higher than that.

6. Malthus was not only a demographer but a _____.

7. Currently, the Canadian population is growing at slightly more than one percent per year. Most of that increase is due to _____, not immigration.

8. Most immigrants to Canada do not go to the empty lands of the West but to _____, _____, and _____.

9. Overall, about ____ percent of Canada's population lives on a small percent of its land, specifically the Windsor-Quebec City corridor and the four Western cities.

10. _____ determinants of fertility include abortion, contraception, and breastfeeding.

11. A _____, not industrialization or transportation, was the most basic factor that allowed the initial growth of cities and urbanization.

12. For sexually active unmarried women, _____ is the most common form of contraception, while for married people it is _____.

13. For older women, _____ and _____ were important factors in explaining variations in fertility. Among young women today education is key.

14. An _____ is the main factor that allows the growth of suburbs on vacant land.

15. The change from a young to an old national population is accounted for primarily through _____ fertility and then a stabilization of the birth rate at a _____ level.

16. All people who share a common starting point, like being born in the 1980s, are part of a particular _____.

Answers

KEY TERMS AND DEFINITIONS

1. total fertility rate
2. period measures
3. expectation of life at birth
4. positive checks
5. dependency ratio
6. age-specific fertility rates
7. crude birth rate
8. migration
9. preventive checks
10. demographic transition theory
11. rate of natural increase
12. age-specific death rates
13. demography
14. crude death rate
15. population pyramid
16. cohort measures
17. life table

SELF-QUIZ

1. d
2. c
3. a
4. b
5. e
6. c
7. e
8. a
9. e
10. c
11. d
12. b
13. c
14. c
15. b

FILL IN THE BLANKS

1. fertility, mortality, migration
2. fecundity
3. fertility, mortality
4. high, low, rapid; low, low, low
5. 30
6. minister
7. natural increase
8. Toronto, Vancouver, and Montreal
9. 75
10. Proximate
11. food surplus
12. the pill, sterilization
13. religion, ethnicity
14. improved transportation system
15. declining, low
16. cohort

CHAPTER 16

Social Change

OBJECTIVES

1. To understand how human societies have changed over the past 10 000 years, from gathering and hunting to industrial.

2. To be familiar with different theories of social change: evolutionism, developmental theories, historical materialism, the Weber thesis, and the state theory of modernization.

3. To learn something about specific changes, including greater equality, the decline of the traditional family, postmodernism, postmaterialism, and globalization.

KEY TERMS AND DEFINITIONS

1. _____: normlessness.

2. _____: Toennies' term meaning society or association, for the cold impersonal, and self-interested social relations of industrial cities.

3. _____: the control or exploitation of one country by another, often by conquest.

4. _____: the theory that argues that the limited development of the third world is a consequence of third world factors such as traditional cultures, capital shortages, lack of technological expertise, etc.

5. _____: integration based upon similarity.

6. _____: Toennies' term meaning community, describing the warm and intimate social relations he saw as being found in agrarian communities prior to industrialization.

7. _____: eighteenth-century movement championing free speech, freedom of conscience, equal rights, empiricism, skepticism, and reason.

8. _____: integration based on cooperation of different parts.

9. _____: the approach that divides countries into core, periphery, and semi-periphery and sees countries as forming a unified system.

10. _____: the organization in a society that has a monopoly on the legitimate use of force.

11. _____: a result of different rates of change in a society.

12. _____: Innis' idea that the economic, political, and cultural formation of Canada was shaped by its geography and the raw materials available for export; the result was our vulnerability to foreign metropolitan centres.

13. _____: an intellectual movement advocating moral relativism; it promotes the idea that science and culture are often forms of domination and control.

14. _____: the adoption of an innovation by a society that did not create it.

15. _____: theoretical perspective maintaining that social change occurs to promote survival and to help societies reproduce themselves, via complex social structures, powerful armed forces, and large populations.

16. _____: one that takes into consideration the effects of the biophysical environment, a society's subsistence technology, and interaction between societies.

17. _____: a perspective claiming that social change results primarily from economic factors, often associated with Marx and Engels.

18. _____: the view that holds that international free trade, privatization, minimal government regulation provide optimal conditions for economic development in all countries, wealthy or poor.

19. _____: those that place a high priority on non-material things such as self-expression, participation in decision making, self esteem, and intellectual development.

20. _____: those that place a high priority on economic and physical security.

21. _____: social improvement; also the belief that social change ultimately results in better social conditions.

22. _____: the formalization procedures that give actors a measure of predictability in the outcomes of their actions.

23. _____: the theory that modern capitalism emerged in Europe because the governments were relatively weak there.

24. _____: perspective that underdevelopment in the Third World is a result of its domination and exploitation by rich industrialized nations.

SELF-QUIZ

1. Although there was great diversity among gathering and hunting societies, they were generally all of the following, except:

    a) spiritual
    b) egalitarian
    c) nomadic
    d) small
    e) sharing

2. Exploitation and pronounced inequalities had their origin in _____ societies.

    a) farming
    b) industrial
    c) postindustrial
    d) hunting and gathering
    e) gathering and hunting

3. In farming societies, women generally had _____ power than men.
    a) more
    b) the same amount
    c) it depended; economically women had power, over defence, not
    d) less
    e) more institutionalized

4. The Enlightenment was not marked by

    a) skepticism
    b) reason
    c) observation
    d) pro-monarchy sentiment
    e) challenge

5. For Spencer, the order for the evolution of society is from

    a) industrial to postindustrial
    b) industrial to militant
    c) farming to hunting and gathering
    d) complex to ever simpler forms
    e) militant to industrial to artistic and intellectual

6. Which order is chronologically correct?

    a) hunting/gathering, agrarian, horticultural, industrial
    b) horticultural, hunting/gathering, agrarian, industrial
    c) hunting/gathering, horticultural, agrarian, industrial
    d) agrarian, hunting/gathering, horticultural, industrial
    e) none of the above

7. Anomie is more likely to be found in which type of society?

   a) mechanical
   b) organic
   c) geselleschaft
   d) gemeinschaft
   e) b and c

8. The _____ approach emphasizes change, conflict, and eventually demise.

   a) positive
   b) dialectical
   c) evolutionary
   d) neo-evolutionary
   e) materialist

9. The religion that Weber saw as the basis for the creation of capitalism is

   a) Methodism
   b) Lutheranism
   c) Roman Catholocism
   d) Calvinism
   e) Judaism

10. A discussion of patricians and plebeians and of lords and serfs is part of whose theory of social change?

    a) Comte
    b) Spencer
    c) Weber
    d) Marx and Engels
    e) a and b

11. The "Great Disruption" does not encompass increasing

    a) crime
    b) divorce
    c) equality
    d) number of births out of wedlock
    e) individualism

12. There are no facts, only interpretations is a tenet of

    a) postmaterialism
    b) evolutionism
    c) postmodernism
    d) anomie
    e) positivism

FILL IN THE BLANKS

1. The study of social change, perhaps more than any other area of sociology, requires a _____ or international focus.

2. One major difference between earlier foraging societies and industrial societies is the existence of the formal _____ today, that body which can legitimately use force.

3. Because hunting and gathering societies had virtually no _____ , there was little inequality or exploitation.

4. Spencer and the term survival of the fittest are part of _____ theory.

5. For Spencer, the growing differentiation and integration of society results primarily from _____ .

6. _____ technology is that needed to acquire the basic necessities of life.

7. The big difference between agrarian and horticultural societies involves the use of the _____ .

8. Canada's exportable fish, furs, lumber, and minerals were termed _____ by Innis.

9. For Comte the three eras of social development were the theological, metaphysical, and finally scientific or _____ stage.

10. Community, kin, friendships, and belonging marked Toennies _____ .

11. Historical materialism emphasizes material or _____ factors in explaining social change.

12. Weber disagreed with Marx and suggested that other factors, not just economic ones, explain social change. The one he chose to emphasize was _____ and more specifically the _____ .

Answers

KEY TERMS AND DEFINITIONS

1. anomie
2. geselleschaft
3. imperialism
4. modernization theory
5. mechanical solidarity
6. gemeinschaft
7. Enlightenment
8. organic solidarity
9. world system theory
10. state
11. structural lag
12. staples thesis
13. postmodernism
14. diffusion
15. evolutionism
16. ecological-evolutionary theory
17. historical materialism
18. neo-liberalism
19. postmaterialist values
20. materialist values
21. progress
22. rationalization
23. state theory of modernization
24. dependency theory

SELF-QUIZ

1. b
2. a
3. d
4. d
5. e
6. c
7. e
8. b
9. d
10. d
11. c
12. c

FILL IN THE BLANKS

1. comparative
2. state
3. surplus production
4. evolutionism
5. conflict
6. Subsistence
7. plow
8. staples
9. positive
10. gemeinschaft
11. economic
12. religion, Protestant ethic

NOTES

NOTES

NOTES

NOTES

NOTES

NOTES

NOTES

NOTES

NOTES

NOTES